Praise for *Cultivating a Classroom of Calm*

"Meredith's years of experience as an educational leader, deep knowledge and understanding of student behavior, and passion for creating the conditions for all students to thrive come together in her work, and the result is a must-read for today's educator. Meredith weaves a quality of relatability and authenticity throughout her work that allows the reader to connect with the content in a way that personalizes the experience. The need to cultivate a calmer classroom is greater now than it has ever been, and Meredith has captured actionable strategies backed with sound research to equip teachers with a deeper understanding of student behavior and practical tools to empower them to make their classrooms a place of learning and acceptance. Today's teachers need this, and Meredith has delivered!"

—**Kristen Canning**, Elementary Instructional Director,
Frederick County (MD) Public Schools

"Every educator, regardless of experience level, should read this book as a reminder of why we are in this field of work: the children. *Cultivating a Classroom of Calm* provides the reader with effective tips and strategies that can be implemented in a classroom immediately to create an optimal learning environment for students. Whether you are teaching PK or AP Government, this book will help you make a huge impact in the educational journey of your students."

—**Jennifer Perry**, Elementary School Quality Specialist,
Henrico County (VA) Public Schools

"Like a teacher's smile from across the room, Meredith McNerney helps educators feel seen as she normalizes emotion as part of every classroom/school experience. From concept to application, this resource honors every beautiful and challenging nuance in the creation of calm."

—**Daryl Howard**, PhD, Equity Specialist,
Montgomery County (MD) Public Schools

"An extremely timely book on tactics and strategies to calm the classroom from internal and external stressors. Meredith McNerney has her pulse on factors that impact everyday teaching and has developed a comprehensive approach to recognizing and defusing stress inducing triggers."

—**Chavaughn Jones-Black**, Montgomery County (MD) Public School (MCPS),
Restorative Justice Coach, Adjunct Professor of DeVry University

Cultivating
a Classroom *of*
Calm

ASCD MEMBER BOOK

Many ASCD members received this book as a
member benefit upon its initial release.

Learn more at: **www.ascd.org/memberbooks**

Cultivating *a* Classroom *of* Calm

How to Promote Student Engagement and Self-Regulation

MEREDITH M^cNERNEY

ascd

Arlington, Virginia USA

2800 Shirlington Road, Suite 1001 • Arlington, VA 22206 USA
Phone: 800-933-2723 or 703-578-9600 • Fax: 703-575-5400
Website: www.ascd.org • Email: member@ascd.org
Author guidelines: www.ascd.org/write

Richard Culatta, *Executive Director*; Anthony Rebora, *Chief Content Officer*; Genny Ostertag, *Managing Director, Book Acquisitions & Editing*; Stephanie Bize, *Acquisitions* Editor; Mary Beth Nielsen, *Director, Book Editing*; Megan Doyle, *Editor*; Thomas Lytle, *Creative Director*; Donald Ely, *Art Director*; Georgia Park, *Senior Graphic Designer*; Valerie Younkin, *Senior Production Designer*; Kelly Marshall, *Production Manager*; Shajuan Martin, *E-Publishing Specialist*; Christopher Logan, *Senior Production Specialist*; Kathryn Oliver, *Creative Project Manager*

All web links in this book are correct as of the publication date below but may have become inactive or otherwise modified since that time. If you notice a deactivated or changed link, please email books@ascd.org with the words "Link Update" in the subject line. In your message, please specify the web link, the book title, and the page number on which the link appears.

PAPERBACK ISBN: 978-1-4166-3283-2   ASCD product #124016

PDF E-BOOK ISBN: 978-1-4166-3284-9; see Books in Print for other formats.

Quantity discounts are available: email programteam@ascd.org or call 800-933-2723, ext. 5773, or 703-575-5773. For desk copies, go to www.ascd.org/deskcopy.

ASCD Member Book No. FY24-3 (Apr 2024 PSI+). ASCD Member Books mail to Premium (P), Select (S), and Institutional Plus (I+) members on this schedule: Jan, PSI+; Feb, P; Apr, PSI+; May, P; Jul, PSI+; Aug, P; Sep, PSI+; Nov, PSI+; Dec, P. For current details on membership, see www.ascd.org/membership.

Library of Congress Cataloging-in-Publication Data
Names: McNerney, Meredith, author.
Title: Cultivating a classroom of calm : how to promote student engagement and self-regulation / Meredith McNerney.
Description: Arlington, Virginia, USA : ASCD, [2024] | Includes bibliographical references and index.
Identifiers: LCCN 2023054027 (print) | LCCN 2023054028 (ebook) | ISBN 9781416632832 (paperback) | ISBN 9781416632849 (pdf e-book)
Subjects: LCSH: Classroom management—United States. | Behavior modification—United States. | Teacher effectiveness—United States.
Classification: LCC LB3013 .M3875 2024 (print) | LCC LB3013 (ebook) | DDC 371.102/40973—dc23/eng/20231214
LC record available at https://lccn.loc.gov/2023054027
LC ebook record available at https://lccn.loc.gov/2023054028

32 31 30 29 28 27 26 25 24   1 2 3 4 5 6 7 8 9 10 11 12

This book is dedicated to my husband, Mark,
for being the kind of teacher I wish every student could have.

Cultivating
a Classroom *of*
Calm

Preface

From an early age, my daughter dreamed of becoming a teacher. With hope in her eyes, she imagined being the type of teacher who would change lives and become a champion for students who needed her most. I worried that the profession would ultimately let her down and strip her of the innocent joy she experienced when fantasizing about the kind of classroom she would create. After 25 years in public education, I have seen a lot. I had reason to worry because I had lived experience, which told me this was not a decision to take lightly.

Serving in various roles across two districts, most recently having served as principal of a large Title I school, I have witnessed the struggle felt by many teachers. I have felt that struggle myself. We give so much because we care, but there is a cost to caring. The truth is, this work can take a toll on every aspect of our lives because it is the work of the soul. Not only are we emotionally invested in the students we serve, but we also often face unreasonable demands. Many of us are tired of the constant pressure, from parents to politicians, and we are fighting a complex system that needs major repair. So, when my daughter insisted on becoming a teacher, I would look into her hopeful eyes and worry. My husband, Mark, is a Title I middle school teacher and is in the thick of the work every day. We asked ourselves the same tricky question: "Is this the life we want for our daughter?"

I know the 2020s, especially, have been absolutely chaotic for many teachers, and as a result, we are losing teachers every day. But I still believe in our profession. I wrote this book to provide a message of hope to young teachers like my daughter, Kaitlyn, and to veterans like my husband, Mark. I wrote this book for you. Thank you for being a champion to our youth, even when some do not appreciate you. Thank you for staying when you could easily leave. I hope to provide professional and personal lived experiences to encapsulate hopeful messages while offering practical strategies to support our most precious professionals. I believe it is an honor to be a teacher. And I also think it is the most demanding job out there. This book is not meant to sugarcoat the truth. Instead, you will be met with tools and strategies to reignite your spark and honor your work each day. I hope you will find it to be presented in an honest yet hopeful way.

In her senior year of high school, Kaitlyn applied to become a Maryland teaching fellow, which meant she would commit to serving in a Title I school upon graduation. Her application essay moved me. It reminded me of how I felt when I decided to become a teacher. Her young voice caused me to take a deep breath, a long pause, and reflect on what I really believed about the profession. It was her young voice that inspired the idea for this book. Her face lights up when she thinks about becoming a teacher, and I never want that spark to diminish. Mark and I are thrilled for her and her future students. We need teachers like Kaitlyn, and my job is to inspire others to love this profession.

When I was young, my parents used to play teacher with my sister and me. My dad played "Mr. Wilson," a fun, carefree, humorous teacher. My mother played "Mrs. Lynda," a passionate, well-organized, uncompromising instructor. Mr. Wilson's classroom was chaotic. There were science experiments on the floor, sticky notes that labeled objects in different languages throughout the room, and posters of educational memes hanging on the walls. His room was full of life and movement. Mrs. Lynda's room was neat and well-mannered. We wrote poems and personal narratives, learned how to multiply fractions, and memorized the bones in the body. Interrupting discussion was punishable, and movement was rare. The two rooms could not have been more opposite of each other. Yet, I looked forward to attending each. I liked when my dad would pause our work to tell us funny stories. I loved when my mom would explain the moon's phases in a much too complicated yet fascinating way. The characters created by my parents to keep two energetic children entertained unintentionally shaped me into the teacher that I am becoming today.

In my classroom, I will have the joyful spirit of Mr. Wilson with the expectations of Mrs. Lynda. I will connect with my students by sharing silly stories and asking them about their hobbies. I will push them to work hard and fight against the barriers before them. I will teach them that it is better to fail than to not try. I will be their role model, their light, their biggest supporter. With every opportunity I have had to learn about teaching and the education system, my dedication and passion for this profession have only grown wider. What started as a fun game with my parents led to a commitment toward a career that I am learning more about each day.

During my sophomore year of high school, I had the opportunity to become a Faith Formation Teacher for my local church, St. Ignatius of Loyola. This volunteer role was exciting yet intimidating. I questioned my capability to control a classroom of young elementary-aged students at just 15 years old. I then realized that teachers learn by doing. I could read about the different strategies teachers use to create an engaging classroom environment. I could take notes on the things my teachers do to make class enjoyable, but I could never truly learn about this profession by watching; I had to jump in. Each week, my co-teacher and I created a one-hour lesson plan based on the curricula given to us by the church. We made sure each lesson would teach our young students about the Lord in an exciting and understandable way to fuel their curious minds. Every student learns differently. We took this into account when creating our lessons. Visual learners enjoyed when we drew a scene from the Bible, auditory learners thrived when watching educational videos, and our kinesthetic learners worked best when completing hands-on activities.

One of the most prominent challenges teachers face is classroom management. I saw firsthand how difficult it can be to control a classroom filled with life, energy, and distractions. To encourage positive behavior, the students came up with a list of shared expectations and were reminded of them daily. In some instances, I had to pull a child aside to discuss their inappropriate behavior. We would come up with solutions together for how the child could have better handled the situation. By doing this, they learned self-control strategies they could use the next time they encountered a frustrating situation. We would also reward the students with a game, free draw time, or a dance party at the end of each class if they proved they earned it. We would give shout-outs throughout the day that encouraged them to keep working hard and stay on task as they worked toward their reward. On the days when they did not earn the reward, the students would openly discuss the areas they felt they needed to improve on. This taught them that mistakes are inevitable but growth happens when we reflect on and learn from those mistakes.

Throughout this experience, I grew a greater understanding of the need to effectively communicate with families outside of the classroom. When a classroom involves families in their students' education, it helps build a strong support system for every learner. To achieve this, I sent weekly emails to families regarding the classroom agenda and important updates, along with positive messages detailing their students' success in the classroom. For the next year, I continued as a Faith Formation Teacher and adjusted to fit the online schedule as the pandemic temporarily shut down our church. I had to learn how to do what all teachers do best; adapt to change. I found new, creative online tools to teach our students. I was lively and silly through the screen. I made sure we created a classroom environment where everyone felt welcomed, even in a virtual setting.

Dedicated teachers jump at the opportunity to learn more about the profession. They do not let their fear of failure stop them from becoming the teacher they wish to be. I have a passion for teaching, and through experience, I am continuing to learn about the ins and outs of this complex, hectic, and rewarding profession.

One of the biggest lessons I have learned is that all students are capable of success. Most of our 2nd graders are below grade level. Many of them are English language learners, and a handful of them have learning disabilities, such as ADHD. I have also seen some of my students struggle with anxiety and fear of failure. Trauma outside the classroom, such as losing their house to a fire and inappropriate contact with adults, has affected my students firsthand. Even while facing heavy battles, my students are capable. They are capable of improving their reading and writing skills. They are capable of scoring high on their math tests. They are capable of believing in themselves. We give our students accommodations and scaffolds, but we never water down the content. We encourage and expect our students to try their best, even if that leads to an incorrect answer. We teach them self-regulation strategies, such as deep breathing, when they feel overwhelmed. Teachers should be a positive light for their students. They should be the ones to encourage their class to work hard and achieve their goals. I always tell my students that the words "I can't" are not allowed in our classroom. I encourage them to ask questions, but I allow them to struggle. I want them to take a few minutes to work out the problem before immediately asking for help. When they do this, they discover they know more than they thought they did.

As a student who was once insecure and unsure of myself, I understand how it feels to sit in class confused. I tell my students this. I relate to them. I also push them to fight against the voice in their head that tells them they are not smart enough, because they are smart enough. Every child deserves a fair and equitable education. With this mindset, I plan to be an advocate for all of my future students, no matter their ethnicity, socioeconomic status, disability, gender, sexual orientation, etc. I will push them to work hard and never give up on themselves. I will do the same. I will never give up my passion for inspiring and educating our youth.

I will be the first to admit that teaching in a 50 percent or more FARMS school is a daunting task. I grew up with two parents who have worked in the education system and in Title I schools for most of their professional lives. I grew up watching the great effort and determination it takes to be a teacher in a Title I school. But I also grew up watching my parents connect with students who sometimes feel disconnected from the outside world. All teachers are superheroes, regardless of where they teach. However, teaching in a Title I school places extra pressure on teachers to pull every child out of an unfair system. I am willing to take on that task.

I cannot be naive. Most of my students will struggle to fight against the unfair challenges set up against them, and some may never come out on the other side, but I will be their lead commander in the fight. I will create a classroom environment that praises risk takers and does not shame wrong answers. I will ask them about their dreams because I am genuinely curious. I will set up a food drawer for students to grab snacks when they are hungry. I will do everything in my power to help them believe in themselves. I will write them encouraging notes and tell them to repeat positive affirmations to themselves, because if they do not believe in themselves, it does not matter how much I believe in them. I will not be a perfect teacher. I will make mistakes, and I will fail.

My students will not be perfect. They will make mistakes, and they will fail. Both of these things are perfectly OK. Failure is not negative; rather, it is the stepping stone to success. My students, rich or poor, above grade level or below, confident or insecure, will have a teacher who supports them in all of their endeavors.

From playing teacher with my parents to volunteering as a Faith Formation Teacher to earning an internship in a 2nd grade classroom, my passion for teaching has been a constant in my life. I want to be a changemaker. I want to make a difference in the world of education. I want to inspire the younger generation to attack their dreams. My determination and work ethic will help guide me along the way, but it is the success stories of my students that will keep me fighting.

—Kaitlyn McNerney,
Maryland Teaching Fellow, Towson University

1

What Is a
Calmer Classroom?

Mrs. Finch stands outside her classroom greeting students like it's the first day of school, every day, with the same energy in February as she had in September. She welcomes each student by name, greeting them with a fist bump or high-five, repeatedly using language such as "I am happy to see you, Amyia!" or "So glad you are here, Diego!" Students light up around her, and in her room everyone belongs. The adults who enter her room feel this energy too. She is unapologetically kind and genuinely concerned about fostering a culture of calm.

She is not quiet; that is not what makes her calm. In fact, her voice is filled with so much energy, she can often be heard down the hallway. No, calm is not about silence in her room. Calm is an internal feeling that penetrates anyone in her presence because, in her room, you know you belong. Mrs. Finch's calm classroom is active, lively, fun, and intentionally structured. But most of all it is safe and inclusive.

In a calmer classroom, students are engaged; trauma-informed practices are applied; there is a balance between empathy and accountability; and adults and children apply strategies to stay emotionally regulated.

Intentionally cultivating a classroom of calm begins within. Calm is a choice. It requires us to be emotionally aware of what is within our locus of control and what is not. You cannot eradicate poverty in the school community or change a poorly managed school. In fact, in many cases, there is a lot that is out of your control. There will always be a lot of hallway chatter. It is often negative and toxic. Empower yourself by clarifying what is within your control and barricade yourself from the rest of the noise around you.

What Does It Mean to Cultivate a Classroom of Calm?

To begin with, we will define what it means to *feel* calm (see Figure 1.1). Calm is a state of feeling relaxed, at ease, or without stress. In order to achieve this feeling, we must be aware of our own feelings and understand how to manage our emotions. We need to feel a sense of belonging and experience human connection. Without having these basic human needs met, it is impossible to remain calm at school or in our personal relationships (Won et al., 2018).

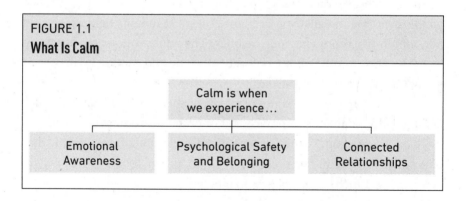

FIGURE 1.1
What Is Calm

Calm is when we experience...

Emotional Awareness

Psychological Safety and Belonging

Connected Relationships

Keep in mind, our sense of calm is constantly changing. We can go from feeling calm one minute to feeling completely overwhelmed the next. Some days we feel calmer than others, and in some environments, it is easier to remain calm, while in other spaces, it is almost impossible to feel calm. What feels calm to me is different from what feels calm to you. Therefore, cultivating a calmer classroom is not achievable without *practice*. Calmer classrooms are cultivated through intentional teacher moves. We cannot remove stress from our schools entirely, but we can intentionally work to cultivate calm by using specific tools and strategies inside our classroom walls (see Figure 1.2). In this way, we practice cultivating calm to create classrooms that are conducive to learning.

Throughout this book, we will further examine what it means to *feel* and *practice* calm. We will examine various strategies and tools to help you choose calm and cultivate calm among your students. Calm students equal calm educators.

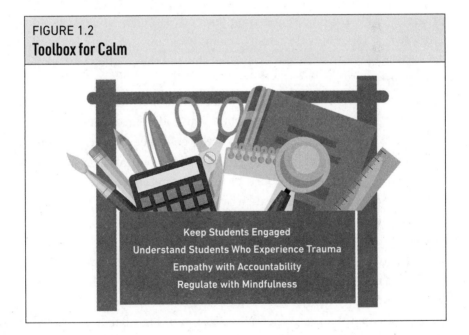

FIGURE 1.2
Toolbox for Calm

Keep Students Engaged
Understand Students Who Experience Trauma
Empathy with Accountability
Regulate with Mindfulness

Anything but Calm

If many of us agree that a calmer classroom is ideal, why is it so hard to maintain a sense of calm in our schools? All too often educators are expected to show up and teach in environments where staff mental health is not prioritized and student mental health is not taken seriously. Our profession is often unpredictable and filled with chaos. The demands placed on educators are at an all-time high, and many of us have experienced burnout over the last few years (Kasalak & Dagyar, 2022). Now we are seeing record numbers of teachers quitting the profession or counting down their years until retirement.

One of the things that we know about the human brain is that when pushed too far, performance suffers. If we want to cultivate calmer classrooms, we have to be aware of how detrimental it is to remain in a state of frustration. "When we pile more on, we falsely believe more will be accomplished" (Thomas et al., 2019). All too often we place new initiatives, new programs, and new requirements on teachers. It builds up and piles on in a way that interrupts the sense of calm. We know that there is a direct correlation between a teacher's sense of calm and the creation of a calmer classroom.

When you open your email and feel inundated with more to-dos or unwanted invites to meetings, when you find yourself unexpectedly engaging in a frustrating conversation with a colleague, or when a student disrupts your lesson, a physiological reaction in your body occurs. Your brain literally secretes hormones to tell your nervous system to fight, flight, or freeze. What we do next has a lot to do with our ability to return to calm. Without strategies, a plan, or an understanding of why we feel this way, we can suffer for a much longer time.

How do teachers possibly cultivate calm within their classrooms when it feels like many schools are falling apart? In this book, we will not diminish burnout felt by teachers (Kasalak & Dagyar, 2022), but we will focus on what we can manage inside any classroom. Let's begin to examine the science behind calm and the best approaches for maintaining a calm classroom.

Emotional Awareness Cultivates Calm

Right now, take a moment to select two words that describe how you're feeling as we begin to explore what it means to cultivate a classroom of calm. This self-awareness practice is essential in order to notice what it feels like when we are calm and when we are not. By simply naming how we are feeling, we begin the process of regulating our emotions (Kopelman-Rubin et al., 2020). Not only is it an important tool for reflection, but being able to name our emotions helps us realize that we can often feel two opposing emotions at the same time—such as calm and unsure, happy and nervous, or sad and hopeful. When we realize that our emotions are normal, we are better able to manage them, which is the first step to cultivating a calm classroom.

When we talk about creating calmer classrooms, we really need to understand the connection between calmer classrooms and social emotional learning (SEL). The Collaborative for Academic, Social, and Emotional Learning (CASEL) defines social emotional learning as "an integral part of education and human development. SEL is the process through which all young people and adults acquire and apply the skills, knowledge, and attitudes to develop healthy identities, manage emotions, and achieve personal and collective goals" (CASEL, 2015). This also requires an ability to feel and show empathy for others, which comes from our own emotional awareness.

Emotional awareness specifically refers to our ability to recognize and manage emotions. When we are self-aware, we are able to name our strengths and understand our challenges and therefore check in with ourselves to assess how we're feeling. Inside a calm classroom, we are able to support students through a big emotion and help them reflect on their feelings in a way that validates their experience.

We can all relate to the experience of something happening to us that causes our bodies to feel an uncomfortable sensation. When I am triggered by an unwanted comment, an unfavorable criticism, or a student behavior that is disruptive, my body takes the emotion inward and creates a sensation I feel in my neck and shoulders. Children and adults need to understand that when our bodies suspect a threat, we react by releasing stress hormones like cortisol and adrenaline (Rosanbalm et al., 2021). Even if we are not in physical danger, our body immediately goes into protective mode, and our thoughts, emotions, and physical reactions are just as strong as if we were being harmed. Simply put, our initial reaction is often followed by subsequent emotions, referred to as meta-emotions (Gottman et al., 1996). It is important to understand that this initial sensation is not your fault; it is your body's natural response to an unwanted event.

Without managing our body's response system, elevated stress hormones can affect our ability to sleep, cause us headaches and stomach pains, and even increase feelings of anxiety and defensiveness (Rosanbalm et al., 2021). This reaction also greatly affects our ability to concentrate, and we may find ourselves feeling more impulsive or forgetful. We can apply strategies when we first experience a reaction to a perceived threat, but this requires us to be emotionally aware of our triggers and big feelings. Intentionally pausing when a trigger occurs helps us begin to settle the elevated hormones so that we can return to a state of calm.

When we get angry, a group of cells in our brains are activated, but new research has helped us understand that it takes only 90 seconds for that circuit to relax if we choose calm (Bolte Taylor, 2021). Taking a meta-moment is an intentional pause that allows us to think before reacting; the key is to notice how you feel and become more self-aware as to why you are upset (Brackett, 2020). When you stop and apply intentional strategies, you are more likely to reclaim your sense of calm rather than spiral into a dark place. Our bodies feel this reaction for extended periods of time because we are choosing to repeat the thought or ruminate on what is upsetting when we should be intentionally choosing to let it go.

In order to cultivate calm, we must understand that safe and supportive learning environments are not free of frustrating moments. At times, student behavior will disappoint you and potentially rob you of your sense of calm. School policies may frustrate you and rob you of your sense of calm. Parents may criticize you and rob you of your sense of calm. Instead of wishing for your body to stop reacting when you are triggered, embrace your body's response system because it is a signal that you feel unsafe. Then apply an intentional strategy to regulate yourself and choose calm. We can use intentional strategies to cultivate emotional awareness.

1. Q-TIP

We have to give ourselves space and validate that we all have feelings and experiences that can be frustrating when working with students who display unfavorable behavior. We must learn to not take it personally. There is a great acronym for this, Q-TIP, which is "Quit Taking It Personally." If the end goal is to cultivate calm, even in difficult situations, we need to recognize when we are taking something personally.

2. Know Your Triggers

We have all been in situations where we started the day feeling calm and then a trigger happens. If we know the types of behaviors, interactions, or situations that tend to upset us the most, then we can overcome our initial reaction because we know what to expect from ourselves.

Pencil tapping, destroying property, eye rolling, or interruptions are all behaviors that have the potential for us to lose our sense of calm. The more our feelings escalate, the more our students around us can become escalated (Burgess et al., 2018). It's important to understand that when unwanted behavior occurs, we have to think about intervening in a way that is safe and calm. Avoid getting in a student's face or engaging in arguments or sarcasm or humiliation techniques as a way to deal with your frustration. If we're being overly defensive or shouting and raising our voice, then we're going to inevitably escalate behavior and lose calm in our classrooms.

Instead, we must think about our nonverbal cues, our tone, and our word choice. All students, regardless of behavior, deserve dignity. Remember to take a deep breath when you feel triggered so that you can respond with brief and consistent strategies rather than react in a way that causes further damage. Something as simple as remembering to breathe at the first sign of getting agitated will help you gain present-moment awareness and restore balance (Metz et al., 2013).

3. Body Scan

When we as humans are emotionally escalated, our prefrontal cortex is unable to do its job (Kopelman-Rubin et al., 2020). The prefrontal cortex is the part of the brain in which we do our best thinking. When we are upset, our emotions take over and our emotional center, the limbic system, is activated. When this happens, we can lose our ability to respond, think, or act rationally and calmly.

A body scan is an effective way to calm ourselves when we are emotionally escalated. Notice how you're feeling in the present moment from the top of your head down to your toes in order to connect with the present moment (Schure et al., 2008). This practice is a popular and effective form of guided meditation. When I engage in a body scan, I start at the top of my head and work slowly down to my toes to understand how I'm feeling and connect with the sensations in my body. I notice tension being held in my neck and shoulders. In order to release it, I intentionally put breath into the area of tension, without judging myself for how I am feeling.

4. Rose, Bud, Thorn

One strategy to build emotional awareness is "Rose, Bud, Thorn," which is a popular tool in many education circles to reflect on areas of "success, potential growth, and opportunities for improvement" (University of Colorado–Boulder, 2022, para. 1). A *rose* is essentially a success or something that you're excited about or proud of. A *thorn* is a challenge in your life. It is something that you are currently struggling with, or it is a perceived difficulty. A *bud* is a potential that you see—whether it is something that you feel hopeful about or a belief that a particular situation will get better. This strategy is helpful for teachers who want to engage in reflection and create a sense of inner calm; it acknowledges that we can be both proud and anxious or hopeful and worried at the same time. This is also useful when working with students to help them cultivate their own emotional awareness.

Psychological Safety and Belonging

Psychological safety and belonging are basic human needs, and they lay the foundation for a calmer classroom (Furrer & Skinner, 2003). Studies show a sense of belonging is an important factor in students' learning and academic attainment. "When students do not feel accepted and connected at school, they are more likely to drop out of school" (Won et al., 2018). In order to open students up to learning, they must feel psychologically safe at school, which comes from our need for relatedness (Won et al., 2018). Students' perception of the classroom culture, which is often based on their relationship with their teacher, is strongly correlated to student self-esteem and mastery of goals (Patrick et al., 2007). Therefore, being accepted and feeling valued affects motivation.

Self-regulated behavior fosters a sense of calm. Students' efforts to regulate their behavior are closely linked to their perception of how much they are included and valued in the classroom (Won et al., 2018). Therefore, if we want to cultivate calm, we must prioritize psychological safety and belonging.

There is a significant correlation between educator beliefs and expectations and how students perform (Furrer & Skinner, 2003). What we believe about our students directly correlates with what students believe about themselves, which affects their self-efficacy. Rosenthal and Jacobsen first introduced this as the Pygmalion Effect in 1968 to demonstrate the impact of teacher expectations on student performance. Researchers at an elementary school measured teacher beliefs about students and student performance, and they used a pretest to measure actual student achievement. Then, without actually using the results of the test, they randomly told teachers which of their students were potentially gifted. Teachers believed they were high scoring, regardless of their score on the pretest. Several months later, data revealed that those students scored significantly higher on the posttest compared to their peers. According to Rosenthal and Jacobsen (1968), success can be attributed to their teachers' belief in their potential.

This experience still holds value today. It is no surprise that teachers have a great influence over their students. Therefore, it is essential to approach this work with an asset-based mindset. Our students can sense how we feel about them, and their performance is positively or negatively affected as a result.

Engaging in hallway chatter or griping about students fosters negativity. While everyone needs to vent or get things off their chest at times, staff who engage in conversations that reflect negativity toward students are essentially establishing a culture of failure. Focusing on what is not working fosters more negativity. This lack of asset-based thinking disrupts our sense of calm.

The language we use with students matters too. Our word choice, body language, and overall affect translates into messages received by students. Students are empowered when their teachers tell them that they are capable and valued. But they can also feel it when these words are no longer genuine. It is important to set high expectations for students rather than focusing on what they cannot do yet.

We can use intentional strategies to cultivate psychological safety and belonging.

1. Model Vulnerability

Resilience is built during times of uncertainty. We learn more about strengths, skills, and abilities during times of stress. This is an opportunity for us to model how to handle stress, change, and challenges. It is OK to not be OK all of the time. It is not practical to think that you will always remain calm. Be willing to speak to people who make you feel safe about the areas in life in which you are struggling. Without oversharing, it is OK to tell your students when you are feeling a little off or having a bad day. You can model this form of emotional awareness and build bonds in the meantime. This will help them to see you as a human with emotions just like them.

2. Celebrate Multilingual Learners

I once overheard a teacher say, "I do not let them speak Spanish in my room. I have no idea what they are saying, and we cannot have that." While this teacher did not mean harm, she was essentially denouncing the students' culture and placing a higher value on the dominant language rather than celebrating the linguistic gifts of her students.

Teachers do not need to be bilingual in order to affirm linguistic differences. Instead, allow language differences to be an asset in the classroom. This can be done in various ways, and any effort to honor a student's first language is a step in the right direction. Teachers can allow students to share their ideas in their first language first before writing or speaking in English. Student translators can help with this too. Students should be offered opportunities to write in their first language as a way to process information and as a way to further develop their linguistic gifts. Most important, students should be comfortable using their first language to converse with other students or speak in the language that feels socially comfortable and safe.

There is no evidence to support an English-only mindset. In fact, research shows bilingualism improves executive functioning skills like attention, increases creative problem solving, and improves working memory (Grote et al., 2021). The evidence for maintaining and further developing a student's first language not only improves memory and learning but also demonstrates the value placed on a student's culture and identity (Vue et al., 2017).

When I was a principal, 78 percent of my students spoke English as a second language. There was a long-standing tradition to teach English only at the school. Over time, students lost their ability to access their first language, eventually making it hard to communicate within their own families, who primarily spoke Spanish. Our data reflected the need for change, but more important, from an equity standpoint, our students deserved a different approach.

As a result, we started a bilingual/biliteracy program and began to honor their first language rather than diminish it. While it is not always possible to make programmatic changes in your school—to move from monolingual teaching to bilingual teaching—each teacher can make small changes that make a huge impact. It is important to reflect on your current mindset and practices to ensure that students' linguistic assets are seen as a gift rather than something that they need to hide.

3. Affirm Identity Differences

While tolerance of one another is important, it is not enough. Tolerance implies a willingness to put up with someone who is different from us. Affirming someone's identity requires empathizing, engaging, and connecting with a person who is different from us. It is impossible to create a sense of belonging for all students if only some students are valued (Won et al., 2018).

Race, gender, sexual orientation, religious affiliation, and disability status are part of our identity. Identity also includes how we see ourselves, what we think of ourselves, our beliefs, personality traits, how we express ourselves, and more. It is important to understand our own identity. In order to genuinely foster belonging in our classrooms, we must be emotionally engaged adults (Arslan & Allen, 2021).

First, we must understand our own positionality: our social position and power. Our positionality affects how we view the world and how we interact with others. We diminish a sense of belonging if we utilize our positionality as educators to control our students, engage in a power dynamic, or subconsciously determine who belongs based on our own personal identity, beliefs, and preferences (Furrer & Skinner, 2003).

If we truly want to create a culture of inclusivity, we must also consider how our own biases have the potential to affect our beliefs about students (Vue et al., 2017). Most people are scared to talk about biases because they think their biases make them bad people. This is untrue. Even good people have biases, but instead of shying away from our biases, we need to be honest about them so that we do not engage in harmful actions as a result.

Our brains like patterns, and it is often these patterns that have the potential to cultivate a bias. For example, as a child I was sick a lot and required the medical care of several doctors. Based on the pattern of my experiences, I developed a mental picture of a "doctor" as an old white man. As I have intentionally sought to diversify who I receive medical care from today, my mental picture of a doctor has evolved quite a bit.

We might have mental pictures of "Advanced Placement" students or "disruptive" students based on a limited view or lack of experience. Being blind to our biases will only perpetuate racism and discriminatory practices. "Beliefs alone do not result in disparate outcomes" (Furrer & Skinner, 2003). It is our actions based on our beliefs that cause harm. Simply put, if we do not examine how our biases may be negatively impacting typically marginalized students, we will continue the cycle of discrimination in our schools. Antibias education is an enthusiastic acceptance of all children and their families. This includes how we interact with one another with the intentional effort to eradicate prejudice and "the harmful emotional and psychological impacts on children from societal prejudice and bias" (Derman-Sparks & Edwards, 2021, para. 1).

If we cannot admit our biases, we fail to work on understanding how these biases are shaping our judgments—often unintentionally. If we open ourselves up to exploring the biases we have and how they may have been formed, we can widen our lens and reduce narrow thinking toward others. The key is to ensure we are not acting on our biases or further perpetuating them.

Connected Relationships

Have you ever stopped to think about how your interactions with one student may be affecting another? Both positive and negative interactions elicit a ripple of emotions, but it's not just between the two people interacting. A positive interaction between you and another student is felt by all students because of something called social contagion (Burgess et al., 2018). In fact, social contagion also explains why we might feel upset while witnessing an argument or negative interaction even if the incident has nothing to do with us.

Every child deserves to have a positive, trusting relationship with at least one adult at school. Human connection is a basic need, and without it, it is impossible to experience calm (Zhang et al., 2022). We need human connection in order to be whole. The culture inside a classroom has a lot to do with achievement as well. If a student believes their teacher likes them, they perform better (Burgess et al., 2018). If they believe their teacher enjoys teaching, they will perform better (Bernstein-Yamashiro & Noam, 2013). If the class community is built on human connection, all students will perform better (Li & Lerner, 2013).

The research goes further to note that teachers who are under an enormous amount of stress will pass that stress on to their students (Burgess et al., 2018); therefore, negative connections can be created. It is reasonable to conclude that teachers' emotions toward teaching have a profound effect on students' emotions and readiness to learn. Contagion plays a huge role in our schools and classrooms. As adults, if we are constantly around negative teammates or we are spending time engaging in damaging hallway chatter, we lose our sense of calm and we pass that negativity on to our students. In order to cultivate calm, we must be careful about who we are spending time with inside and outside school. As humans we are influenced by one another, and our moods are directly translated to our students (King, 2020).

Connected positive relationships—that is, the staff-to-staff, staff-to-student, and student-to-student relationships—are responsible for our ability to experience calm. However, many teachers wonder how they will have time to connect with every student every day. There is good news! Social contagion teaches us that we do not have to have a personal connection to every student every day for a positive connection to be felt (Perry, 2002). For example, correcting a student with dignity will have a positive influence on the rest of the students in the classroom. Small interactions like smiling at a student from across the room will be enough to send a message that they are seen. Your facial expressions and body language can also have a positive influence on the connected relationships in your classroom. Cultivating connected relationships cultivates interdependence in the classroom and plays a large role in the success achieved by the entire class as a whole (Perry, 2002).

We can use intentional strategies to cultivate connected relationships between staff and students and between peers.

1. The Power of Being Seen

When I initially read the article "The Power of Being Seen," I realized the concept of "seeing" all students is simple (Korbey, 2017). We need to know our students, and that goes beyond knowing about their academic achievements or the scores they received on the latest assessment. If emotion and learning are truly connected, then we must understand our students as real people with real interests, backgrounds, and emotions. During a staff meeting, during a team meeting, or on your own, turn your student roster(s) into a checklist. Check off which students the members of your team know by name. Go further to identify three things you want to know about every student, such as their personal interests and their family dynamic. You can consider information such as the following:

- Do we know this student's favorite type of music?
- Does this student have any siblings?
- Is this student involved in any clubs or sports?

Using a checklist format, mark off which questions you can answer about your students or find out who in your department knows that personal information about each student. It is fascinating to see which students are well known and which are not. Compare notes with people who also teach your students. The power of being seen is about intentionally noticing our students, understanding who they are as people outside the academic setting, and creating meaningful connections.

2. Greeting Students at the Door

It's not abnormal for us to feel overwhelmed by the lack of time we have each day or the imposing to-do list that never seems to end. As a result, we may want to catch up on everything that feels urgent. While that is certainly understandable, this often means we are at our desks sending that one quick email rather than setting up the conditions for engagement.

Something as simple as greeting students at the door (i.e., greeting each student by name, with a high-five or a handshake) produces incredible results (Lynass & Walker, 2021). Teachers can expect an increase in engagement by 20 percent between students who are greeted each day compared with those who are not. The data also points out a 9 percent reduction in disruptive behaviors as a result of making this one change (Cook et al., 2018).

Students need to develop a sense of self. Teach them the power of affirming statements that build confidence and self-awareness. For younger students, I would suggest greeting students outside the classroom each morning. Hold up a full-length mirror for students as they enter the classroom and ask them to verbally commit to a kindness affirmation while looking at their reflection. Affirmations might include "I am kind," "I am ready to learn," "I am a good friend," or "I am ready to listen." Of course, these will need to be modeled and practiced. This will set the tone for the day.

With all students, it is important that they are greeted by name. Make eye contact with your students as they enter and consider a nonverbal greeting such as a high-five or fist bump. Insert words of encouragement such as "Ryan, great to see you!" This simple shift does not take time away from your lesson—it will buy you time on your task in the long run. The act of setting the tone at the door will yield surprising benefits. This simple strategy creates a culture in which young people feel valued.

3. Community Circles

Cognitive psychologist Daniel Willingham (2021) argues that teachers should focus more on using questions. He describes how questions light up our brains and help us get curious about what we are learning. Too often, we start class with something that sounds like this: "Come in, take out your notebook, and write 'warm-up' at the top." While we need routines and structure, this approach instantly strips the fun out of learning (Willingham, 2021).

Community circles offer opportunities to build connections among students by making the learning personal. For younger students, it is important to start with simple questions such as "What is your favorite food?" This will get students familiar with the process of taking turns and listening to each other. As your class becomes more familiar with the process, you can ask empathy skill-building questions such as "What do you do when someone gets hurt?" For older students, asking questions related to pop culture, their preferences, or their interests will get them talking.

4. Correct with Care

Throughout every part of your day, be mindful of how you correct students when they make mistakes. If they understand that mistakes are a part of learning and risks are celebrated, then being called on will not feel so scary.

One of the most effective ways to develop a growth mindset in students is to affirm students with positive statements rather than overcorrecting (Bauer et al., 2009). Giving students opportunities to reflect on what they did well is a powerful way to open up a student's brain to feedback and learning. Students are motivated when their past successes are affirmed, which leads to higher self-efficacy when compared to students who receive critical feedback without ample praise (Chung et al., 2021).

As much as possible and as often as possible, allow students to edit, revise, and upgrade their work so that they stay motivated during the learning process. If every assignment is for a grade, or if grades are definitive, it can be hard to bounce back and remain engaged. Students will not see the value in the learning process if a grade remains final and there is never an opportunity to learn from feedback.

When we feel calm, we are at ease. But we know that classrooms are complex and complicated, and oftentimes we are expected to perform under pressure. That is why we have to intentionally cultivate calm. There are times when being upset is warranted, and we cannot expect ourselves to remain calm at all times. That would be an unfair and unrealistic expectation placed on us. However, we can learn to be calm under pressure.

Throughout the next four chapters, we will examine ways to practice cultivating calm in your classroom. We will examine the research necessary to empower us to remain calm or return to calm when we feel escalated. We will learn practical strategies to help cultivate calmer students. With intentional practice, we can create calmer classrooms and schools to make teaching and learning enjoyable again. Classrooms can be places of healing if we choose calm.

2

Keep Learners Engaged

The first five minutes of class are the same every day. Students walk in and bury their heads in their cell phones. Even though students are reminded to put their phones out of sight, many sneak around to use them anyway. Students are told to complete the warm-up, and in response, they sluggishly take out their notebooks and give minimal effort to complete the task at hand. During an attempted class discussion, students sit in silence and avoid participating. When called on, they make excuses for why they did not complete the previous night's reading, making it impossible to engage in the discussion questions. Later during an exam, a student whispers to the person next to them to borrow an eraser. They pass the eraser back and forth. It seems plausible there is cheating happening, but it is hard to confirm.

Does any of this resonate with you? We have all encountered students who seem apathetic. I conducted an informal survey of 30 teachers who were asked, "How does it make you feel when students are disengaged?" Overall teachers used words like "It makes me feel frustrated, depressed, discouraged." Several teachers internalized disengagement, stating they felt "like a failure" or told themselves "I must not be a very good teacher."

A lack of student engagement invades our sense of calm. Internal or external chaos occurs in our minds or can be visibly seen in our classrooms when students lack engagement. Simply put, a sense of calm and student engagement go hand in hand.

But to be clear, silence does not necessarily equate to a classroom of calm. Calm classrooms are not places in which we celebrate hearing a pin drop. In fact, the opposite is true. Calm classrooms are places in which learning is occurring and students are engaged in discourse, sharing their ideas and collaborating to push through a productive struggle.

Inside calm classrooms students are actively engaged in the learning process. But how do we cultivate a learning culture when some students seem to be completely checked out?

To begin with, we must understand how learning occurs. Cognition happens in the prefrontal lobe, known as the executive state, which is the part of our brain that is asking, "What can I learn today?" (Steinberg, 2015). As humans, we are wired to learn. However, adversity, distractions, competing interests, or witnessing a fight between parents before school all disrupt engagement.

Many students and adults are coming to school vulnerable. We can all remember a time when we walked into a space and felt unsafe. When this happens, the lower part of our brain, the brainstem, is activated and asking, "Am I safe?" The only way to calm the brain stem from being activated is to create a safe environment. In this way, emotion and learning are completely connected. If students feel safe, they are better primed for academic achievement and cognitive engagement.

Engagement also occurs in the limbic system. When the limbic system is activated, it is asking, "Am I accepted?" (Steinberg, 2015). We all want to feel that we are accepted for who we are. If we do not feel accepted, we are robbed of our sense of calm and, therefore, we cannot learn. Social engagement is necessary to ensure we feel accepted by our peers and the adults around us (King, 2020).

When students are no longer cognitively engaged, we blame them for not doing the work or participating in the lesson. We may think of them as lazy or unwilling to put in the effort. However, we often miss the big picture. How students behave, feel, and think is infused into every aspect of engagement, making it impossible to separate students' behavior, emotion, and social interactions from cognition. In reality, each of these is dynamically interrelated (Won et al., 2018).

In order to learn, we must be calm. Even the best teachers struggle to engage all students because when a student is under stress—no longer calm—it is almost impossible for learning to occur (Perlman & Pelphrey, 2011).

Calm is cultivated through safety and belonging. If the work is too hard, we may start to feel unsafe. If we feel we have nothing to contribute, we may begin to believe we do not belong. When inner calm is lost, academic achievement is impossible.

Simply put, calmer classrooms create the conditions for learning (Mantooth et al., 2021). As a result, if we care about teaching content, we must also care about engaging every facet of the individual student. In order for learning to occur, classrooms must be predictable, safe, inclusive, and fun!

As illustrated in Figure 2.1, creating the conditions for engagement requires a multidimensional approach that connects emotion and learning. Together these dimensions become necessary when creating the conditions for a calmer classroom. When done well, each aspect of engagement works together to cultivate safety and belonging. When we feel safe and when we belong, we are calm. When we are calm, we can learn.

FIGURE 2.1
The Four Dimensions of Engagement

Behavioral	Social	Emotional	Cognitive
Students follow instructions, are prepared for class, and work with intentionality.	Students collaborate to learn and build positive peer relationships.	Students have a sense of belonging, feel a connection to their teacher, and are open to learning.	Students are engaged and willing to invest in their work.

Behavioral Engagement

Behavioral engagement happens when students follow the rules and procedures inside your classroom. When implementing behavior policies, many students will not comply, which is often the moment we begin to lose our calm.

Around the beginning of the 21st century, schools began reporting a decline in respect for authority. Students today no longer automatically comply with the behavioral and academic expectations placed on them (Fredricks et al., 2004). Office referrals, disciplinary reports, and poor attendance rates measure behavioral engagement.

When it comes to behavioral engagement, students are more likely to follow your policies and respect the expectations in your classroom when they feel included in developing them and they can make sense of the "why" behind them. Including students in the development of classroom expectations develops their emotional awareness of how rules and policies can benefit the class to create a calm environment. As we discussed, when we are emotionally aware, we can engage in conversations that are difficult and remain calm while doing so.

An organized classroom is one way to foster more regulated student behavior (Marigen et al., 2022). Students who see other students getting away with unwanted behavior may adopt the same type of behavior. The reverse is also true. When students are highly motivated and engaged in their work, other students are more likely to do the same. Therefore, your expectations need to be very clear and consistent.

Consider examining each part of your day. What is the routine or structure students need to follow in order to be successful? Are these routines clear to students? Is the structure designed in a way that invites everyone to feel safe? Are rules so rigid that only certain students can be successful? Behavioral engagement cannot be separated from emotional engagement. Therefore, as you go through this chapter, it is important to remember the connection between student behavior and their sense of belonging.

Here are four strategies to cultivate calm through behavioral engagement:

1. Classroom Design Affects Behavioral Engagement

The physical attributes of a classroom promote student engagement. Adding symbolic objects to the classroom improves the physical attributes of a space that promotes student engagement. Flexible spaces that are adaptable increase active learning strategies. For example, flexible seating affords movement and leads to greater opportunities for collaboration between students (Rands & Gansemer-Topf, 2017). Wall decor and displayed objects increase positive effect, improving classroom culture. Small changes add up. Even brief and subtle messages come from what we display on our walls. Images of successful people of color signal to students of color that they belong (Cheryan et al., 2014). This small shift can work to reduce achievement gaps.

Rearranging desks to create distinct areas for individual and group work makes collaboration easier. Adding plants, lighting, color, and inspirational posters are simple ways to engage students (Cheryan et al., 2014). Keep in mind as you examine the physical space in your classroom that, when diversity initiatives are framed as all-inclusive (e.g., including displays of both majority and minority groups), this increases student engagement (Cheryan et al., 2014).

2. Examine Your Cell Phone Policy

One area that has become a hot topic is the use of cell phones in schools. In the article "Guiding Students to Develop a Clear Understanding of Their Cell Phone Use," Klein (2022) states, "Banning cell phones from classrooms can backfire, but teachers can help students think critically about this addictive technology" (2022, para. 1). Many teachers are hesitant to address the issue because it is hard to apply consequences and the constant battle is exhausting. Instead, we must create a desire within students to follow your classroom policy. Klein reinforces this by saying that "treating students with empathy and providing respectful, humane solutions to problems like cell phones" may require us to rethink our approach to forced compliance (para. 6).

In order to help students understand the "why" behind your cell phone policy, consider having an open discussion with students at the start of the year (Kolb, 2017). To foster conversation and connection, start by sharing how your cell phone has caused you to become distracted at times, and cite recent research that suggests that even if our cell phone is turned face down, its mere presence can cause us to divide our attention between a task at hand and the constant desire to pick up the phone (Klein, 2022). We can all relate to what our students are experiencing, and most of us will attest to the importance of putting boundaries in place to avoid overusing our cell phones.

The objective is to help students understand your policy and respect it because they have a personal connection to the facts. There are several facts about cell phones that can be shared with students during the discussion:

- Notifications (e.g., vibrations, red dots, flashing lights, banners) cause us to be constantly distracted. The feeling of urgency created by our phones can rewire our brains to constantly need attention (Rosen, 2018).
- This constant attention seeking takes away from our true identity, can distract us from our goals, and may draw us toward negative content (Elhai et al., 2021).
- With a greater focus on mental health, most students are starting to understand how our phones, especially using social media, can cause us to feel disengaged in life and can even lead us to feel insecure and depressed (Liao & Sundar, 2022).

One high school teacher I met recently shared that in one class period she told her students to place a tally mark on the board every time they received a notification of any kind on their phone—every text message or social media notification or anything else. By the end of class there were hundreds of tally marks. Her students were shocked. After that, she clearly articulated her cell phone policy and students followed it because they understood the "why."

Another tip is to consider setting up a cell phone charging station. If you do this, tell students to plug it in, turn the ringer off, and forget about it for the class period. Other simple ideas include using a see-through shoe rack, calculator caddy, or pocket chart for storage during class.

Students respond well to incentives. A teacher shared with me that in her freshman class she would walk around with a giant basket and ask students to place their phone in the basket during the entire class period. If they followed her direction for the week, they were given a treat or some type of incentive.

One of my favorite strategies illuminates the power of relationships. A teacher reported that when he and his co-teacher had a lot of students on their phones, they would take selfies of themselves looking really sad with the students on their phones behind them. When they shared the pictures, the students connected their behavior to the effect on their teachers. He believed the students benefited from understanding the effect their behavior was having on two teachers they liked, and their intention was not to harm them.

Calm classrooms have a strong cell phone policy in place (Elhai et al., 2021). Many policies work, but ultimately you have to find what works best for you and your students. Once you have a policy in place, be careful not to give up on it when one student refuses to comply. Instead, address that separately and decide which battles are worth picking.

3. Utilize Timers to Chunk Assignments

Most teachers have used timers sporadically in their classrooms. Consider using a visual outline of what students are expected to do and match it with a timer. Timers create urgency and can increase motivation—especially when you match the time to an accountability measure. Students may advocate for additional time to complete the task at hand, and it may be appropriate to offer them more time. The point is that timers help students learn to manage their time and work toward an end goal.

This also helps with setting boundaries. When the timer is on, it is work time. When it is possible, allow students a break when the timer goes off. You may even take two minutes for a class movement break or offer students a short moment of downtime to reset before the next part of the lesson. This will foster a great sense of responsibility and teach students to pair hard work with a little self-care.

Timers cultivate calm because they help teachers stay on track and uphold the amount of time they intend to devote to each portion of the lesson (Time on Task, 2004). Most of us can relate to losing track of time during a lesson and then rushing to make up for lost time. This can lead to a feeling of chaos. Instead, a simple timer can cultivate calm.

4. Establish Clear Routines with Habit Stacking

Many experienced teachers know the importance of clear routines. However, it is important to reexamine how routines are taught and reinforced. Students need to know what is expected of them during each portion of the class period or throughout the day. One way to create and maintain effective routines is with habit stacking. Habit stacking helps students build a new habit by stacking it with a habit that is already happening in your classroom.

Add habits like mindful breathing, positive self-talk, affirmations, and quick movement breaks to already established routines. Here are a few examples: *After I hang up my backpack, I will take two deep breaths. After I complete my warm-up, I will write a positive affirmation at the bottom of my paper.* The benefit of habit stacking is connecting to what students already know while enhancing what you would like for them to do.

It's important to remember that focusing on behavioral engagement alone can form a culture of forced compliance, which only lasts so long and ultimately builds a great divide between teachers and students. Forced compliance creates stale and boring classrooms, whereas in a calm classroom, students are willing to take intellectual risks and engage in critical thinking. The next layer of engagement—emotional engagement—works alongside behavioral engagement to foster a personal willingness to follow rules and procedures in a calm classroom.

Emotional Engagement

When students feel a connection to their teacher and peers, they feel calm inside of their classroom. Emotional engagement is the intentional practice of fostering "students' sense of connection to and liking of school" (Markowitz, 2017, p. 1). When students feel calm in their classroom, they internalize the values and goals within the classroom and form healthy relationships. This sense of connection often prevents delinquent behavior and provides students a safe environment to deal with outside stressors.

In the long run, young people who are involved in positive relationships with teachers and peers will maintain a higher sense of self and are more likely to graduate high school and be successful in the future (Wang & Fredricks, 2014). Therefore, it is plausible that calmer classrooms can be cultivated when students are emotionally engaged in learning.

As students move from elementary school to middle school and then to high school, demands of the curriculum shift and the pressure to focus solely on content rises. All the while, older students often need more support from a trusted teacher as levels of engagement decline with age and could lead to higher dropout rates or an increase in delinquent behaviors (Wang & Fredricks, 2014).

If emotion and learning are completely connected, then we are responsible for fostering emotional engagement (Skinner & Pitzer, 2012). If we want to know what students need in order to stay emotionally engaged, then we should ask them (National Education Association, 2012). When we invite student voice in the classroom, we can honor multiple perspectives, practice cognitive empathy (i.e., learn to see through others' eyes), and promote affective empathy (i.e., share others' feelings).

Here are four strategies to cultivate calm through emotional engagement:

1. Collect Student Voice Data

If we really want to connect with our students on an emotional level, then we must prioritize conditions that will enable students to feel safe, supported, and welcome when sharing their perspectives (Cohn-Vargas et al., 2021).

Explain that the questions you are asking will help you learn more about students' perspectives. Generally speaking, when students are asked to share their opinions, it is important to gather information first and then dig into solutions. These skills are essential to cultivating emotional engagement. Also, be careful not to damage relationships in the process by becoming defensive; instead, offer students the choice to opt out of the conversation. If it feels more comfortable, allow students to share their voice anonymously.

Certain questions are more meaningful when a particular opportunity or challenge has already been identified. In order to gather information, formulate one or two open-ended questions. For example, if you are frustrated by your students' unwillingness to collaborate, you might ask, "When you are asked to collaborate with your peers, how do you feel and why?" Because this question is specific to a challenge you have observed, it opens up a host of specific follow-up questions. Be careful not to jump to solution-seeking questions too fast. Formulate follow-up questions to continue to gather information first.

Keep in mind, these conversations can raise more questions than answers. If that happens, consider continuing the conversations on an individual basis or asking additional questions to provide clarity. It may be important to discuss, validate, and then eliminate feedback that is outside your locus of control.

At the same time, student voice offers an opportunity to check our own assumptions and make small shifts to foster a calmer classroom (Cohn-Vargas et al., 2021). We have an opportunity to listen to our students and work together to come up with solutions. After all the information has been gathered and responses outside the locus of control have been eliminated, collaboratively work together to generate a list of solutions.

At the end of the conversation, be sure to thank students for their time and insights. Allow yourself time to process their feedback. Afterward, process the student feedback together and identify next steps.

Overall, remember, students have a voice. If you allow students to use their voice, it will empower them and increase their stake in the learning process. Even simple shifts, like offering more choice of assignments or class projects, can make a huge difference (Zeeman, 2006). Listening to your students will help you understand their perspectives, and it can lead toward greater emotional connections.

2. Utilize the Prompt "I Wish My Teacher Knew"

In her book *I Wish My Teacher Knew*, Kyle Schwartz (2016) describes the moment in which she asked students to fill in the blank in this sentence: "I wish my teacher knew _____." She reports being astounded by the results. While some answers were hilarious, others were downright heartbreaking.

A simple prompt such as this one can open teachers up to understanding the unique realities their students face. While it is impossible to have solutions waiting in response to every heartbreaking circumstance our students are facing, reading their responses builds empathy. Empathy builds emotional connection and fosters inner calm. By hearing the emotional and insightful responses of our students, we are better able to connect with them.

3. Implement the 2 × 10 Strategy

This strategy focuses on relationship building and works best for students who are having a hard time maintaining positive relationships and are exhibiting disruptive behaviors (Wlodkowski, 1983). Ultimately this intervention is targeted for students who need extra emotional support.

To implement, intentionally select a student and set a goal to engage in a two-minute conversation with that student for 10 consecutive school days. These conversations can happen at the beginning or end of a class period (Woolf, n.d.).

This strategy helps students communicate their feelings and emotions and build a deeper connection with a trusted adult. Research shows that implementing the 2 × 10 intervention can lead to significant improvements in individual student behavior and promote a greater sense of connection in the classroom (Galbraith, 2004).

The focus of these conversations should be brief; two minutes or less is ideal. Focus on nonacademic conversations to learn more about your students' interests, and model openness by sharing something personal about yourself.

4. Set Goals with Students

Provide opportunities for students to take ownership of their work by setting goals. Goal setting can be modeled as early as kindergarten. As a class, set small, measurable goals and revisit them often. SMART (specific, measurable, attainable, relevant, and timely) goals are nothing new, but they allow us to focus on short-term, measurable goals that can be tracked and monitored in as little as four to six weeks.

Creating a goal-setting culture can have a profound impact on engagement (Chung et al., 2021). Depending on the age group of your students, goals can be individualized or created collectively and may focus on improved classroom behavior or appropriate individual learning goals. Students will need to make choices about the goals they set. Provide several examples, and allow students to maximize their own agency by letting them set their own meaningful goals. There are also many videos available across many platforms to help students understand the importance of goals and how to write their own.

If you model this process and brainstorm together, students will have a better understanding of the types of goals that are measurable and motivating. Start with short-term goals and eventually consider helping students with goals that are measured over longer periods of time.

Students who set goals have greater self-efficacy and will persevere if they are praised for making progress toward their goal (Chung et al., 2021). Research tells us setting goals and achieving them brings us joy (Hattie & Yates, 2013). Consider how you will display, track, monitor, and celebrate goals with your class. Measuring success in short increments of time will shift the mindset from what students are not yet doing to the possibilities of what they can and will do.

Emotional engagement focuses on the link between emotion and learning, which ultimately cultivates calm. Emotional engagement is about a student's sense of belonging and connectedness to the adult(s) and their peers in the classroom (Furrer & Skinner, 2003). However, if you focus on emotional engagement alone, you run the risk of relying solely on relationships without holding students accountable.

Social Engagement

A student's sense of belonging with teachers or peers precedes school achievement and positive experiences in school (Arslan & Allen, 2021). Social engagement provides the motivational foundation needed to enjoy school and build positive peer relationships (Erwin, 2005). Essentially, students who have strong peer-to-peer relationships are more motivated to engage in their schoolwork (Furrer & Skinner, 2003).

Social relationships built on empathic concern will foster calm. There are several ways to do this, such as setting up a safe culture in which participation feels less scary. This will invite more students to engage with peers. By intentionally utilizing these strategies, students will feel calm when working with peers.

Here are four strategies to cultivate calm through social engagement:

1. Prime Students

Project-based learning (PBL) expert Jorge Valenzuela (2022) makes the point that in order to open the pathways for greater conversation, "some may need time to build a little background knowledge first" (para. 2) because some students are just not comfortable working in a group because they do not feel prepared. As described in Chapter 1, access to background knowledge is a prerequisite to learning. Without intentionally building background knowledge, gaps will widen and many students will never know their full potential. This is especially true as it relates to social engagement. We cannot expect students to engage in a topic if they have not received proper instruction to build their background knowledge.

Another way to prime students is to provide engaging tools that will help them organize their thinking before collaborating with others. It is boring to list ideas in a notebook or use the same old tools. Offer students low-tech tools, such as colorful paper and markers or individual whiteboards, or interactive high-tech tools, such as word clouds or web-based learning platforms. Mixing between low-tech and high-tech tools makes learning fun (Erwin, 2005) and boosts dopamine, which is the pleasure hormone associated with memory.

Providing word banks or using sentence frames to help students recall their ideas is another way to prime students prior to discussion. Teachers often fear using these because they feel these scaffolds decrease rigor. In fact, when used correctly, word banks and sentence frames are a tool to *enhance* rigor. Word banks provide access to key vocabulary and help students recall what they have previously learned so they can think critically about content or academic material. Sentence frames give students an opportunity to articulate what they know while providing a structure to enhance what they could not produce on their own.

If students have something to say, they will be more likely to engage, but if they fear what others think of them, they will shut down. Some students will remain reluctant, but repetition enhances skill. When priming becomes a regular part of preparing for discussions, students should eventually be able to choose priming tools that best help them build confidence prior to working in a group.

2. Foster Peer Relationships

Just like us, students work best with people they know or feel more connected to prior to having to work through a challenge. Wojcicki (2021) shares easy tips for creating a safe culture: "I always started out my new classes with an activity I called 'personality feature.' It was an opportunity for each student to interview one other student in the class and be interviewed." She points out that students work better together when they know each other.

Consider how often groups are reorganized and partners are established. If a certain mix is working, do not be afraid to keep the group intact. While we often think it is better for students to work with all different classmates, inevitably, some combinations of students or partners will work better than others. Test out different ways of priming students, pairing students, and engaging students to promote conversation in your calm classroom.

3. Mix Class Discussion Structures

After priming students for a discussion, create groups of four to six students and give them time to share their thinking. Depending on the topic and age group, provide ample time for the discussion. Rotate only one to two students at time instead of mixing up the entire group.

Alternatively, invite pairs to engage in a discussion. Then pairs can form a group of four. Groups of four can form a group of eight. Continue this process. Eventually the whole class will become one large group.

4. Provide Discourse Stems

Discourse stems help students summarize another person's argument, ask clarifying questions, and express their own opinions. Stems are designed to support a particular aspect of discussion and should be organized according to their purpose. To summarize, consider using "What

I heard you say...." To clarify, consider a stem such as "Tell me more about...." To foster disagreement, consider "My point of view is different because...." This will take modeling and practice, but it is worth the investment of time because discourse stems build confidence and help organize conversation.

Calm classrooms include social engagement that occurs when students collaborate to learn. Collaborative discussions help students build positive peer relationships. Focusing on social engagement alone, however, may cause students to rely heavily on their peers rather than develop their self-efficacy and accountability. Instead, think of social engagement as a way to fuel cognition. As we begin to unpack cognitive engagement, keep in mind that strong social connections foster a culture of learning in a calm classroom (Furrer & Skinner, 2003).

Cognitive Engagement

When our daughters were little, we would often take them to Washington, DC, to explore the museums and monuments. When they were two and three years old, we would walk around and point out important parts of our country's history. They listened for a bit but soon became more interested in ice cream than the monuments. We did not expect them to understand everything we were trying to teach them during the first, second, or even third visit to DC. Over time, learning occurred, but the pathway to their understanding was anything but linear.

Learning involves three key components of the brain: neurons, synapses, and myelin. Neurons are nerve cells in the brain that are "wired" to send messages to other neurons (Sriram, 2020). In the space between neurons, synapses send signals back and forth from one neuron to the next, making the important connections for learning to occur. Myelin protects your nerve cells, and its job is to send messages between your brain and your body. That is why repeated exposure, guided feedback, experiential learning, and hands-on learning are all beneficial to students (Fogarty et al., 2017). When we are engaged cognitively, our synapses light up, allowing neurons to make connections between previously learned and novel information.

Learning is about constructing knowledge through repeated exposure. Just as we would not expect toddlers to comprehend the important aspects of our nation's history, even with two dedicated teachers as their parents, we should not expect students to understand everything right away. However, with constant pressure to cover large amounts of content, we revert to teaching curriculum with a *shove it down as fast as you can* mentality. Instead, learning is about providing students opportunities to engage in a productive struggle so that they experience learning rather than covering curriculum without making it stick (Fogarty et al., 2017).

Because our brains take in so much information throughout the course of each day, inevitably the brain will forget much of what is learned. This is a natural part of the learning process and is surprisingly necessary to prevent overload. If we want to inspire learning and achievement in our classrooms, we must carefully consider how to keep the brain involved in the learning process without overwhelming it with too much content at one time.

Remember, overload leads to a loss of calm. The brain cannot learn when it is overwhelmed. Lessons should be designed to support calm to prime students for learning.

As illustrated in Figure 2.2, in order to foster cognitive engagement, our lesson structure can be broken into three parts.

To create a safe space for all students to engage in the learning process, it is essential to examine how you engage students in the first five minutes of each class period or lesson. During this portion of the lesson, it is important to focus on a low-level cognitive demand to excite and hook the brain rather than overload it. Once students feel safe, we can increase demand. The body of the lesson is where a productive struggle needs to occur. Finally, the role of the optimistic closure is to make learning stick by utilizing strategies that require a medium- or low-level cognitive demand. Using intentional strategies during each part of the lesson will keep the brain interested and involved in learning.

FIGURE 2.2 Lesson Structure		
First Five	**Main Lesson**	**Optimistic Closure**
• This is your hook. • Consider how you create interest or build excitement. • Make learning fun!	• This includes a mix of direct instruction, collaboration, and multiple checks for understanding. • Utilize spacing and intervals to chunk learning and avoid cognitive overload. • Make learning challenging!	• This is a 1–5-minute summary. • Apply strategies to review the most important information. • Utilize checks for understanding. • Make learning sticky!
Low-level demands	High-level demands	Low to medium demands

The First Five Minutes

The first five minutes of every lesson offer an opportunity to make learning fun. Therefore, creating hooks that connect to what students already know is essential to building their confidence before the cognitive demand increases. By keeping the hook of every lesson simple enough for everyone to succeed, you will open students to more difficult challenges later. When students are anxious, unsure, distracted, silently suffering, or outwardly disengaged, priming can prepare them for the rigorous content you need to put in front of them (Kryszewska, 2021).

Setting up the lesson by intentionally focusing on the first five minutes will buy you time later. Hooks are only successful when the assignment feels accessible to all students. Priming students for learning in this way will give them confidence to engage with complex content or engage in a productive struggle that leads to learning.

You do not need to become a world-class entertainer or social media star to hook them. As you read through each of the strategies offered, think about what feels authentic to you. Not all of your attempts to hook learners will work. You will try some strategies and quickly learn when to make modifications, but as you experiment with ideas, you will start to notice which strategies work best as hooks. The first five minutes of every lesson set a tone, and in a calm classroom the first five minutes should be fun!

Here are five strategies to cultivate calm through cognitive engagement during the first five minutes of the lesson:

1. Activate Prior Knowledge … Differently

Like the familiar K-W-L (i.e., what we know, what we want to know, what we learned), activating prior knowledge builds excitement by starting with the familiar. "If students' prior knowledge is faulty (e.g., inaccurate facts, ideas, models, or theories), subsequent learning tends to be hindered because they ignore, discount, or resist important new evidence that conflicts with existing knowledge" (Ambrose & Lovett, cited in Lang, 2021). We can take a long-standing traditional method and customize it to hook students today.

The goal is to create and build excitement prior to the lesson while getting students to recall important information in a unique way. For example, let's suppose you want students to recall the order of operations because these math conventions will be necessary during the lesson. Instead of starting with a traditional warm-up, you could allow teams to watch a two- or three-minute video of a baker using an intentional step-by-step process. Then ask students to compare baking to math. Let teams brainstorm all the connections between math and baking. Give each team a point for each connection and two points if they figure out the connection you are hoping they make. You may say something like "There will be many connections. But there is one that is in alignment with what we have been learning all week. If your team comes up with it, you will earn two points." Give students time to make the connection between ordered steps when baking to the order of operations or conventions in mathematics. This is not about new learning; it is about getting students to remember important information that they will need to access in order to be success-ful with the lesson.

Another way to do this is to state the objective and ask what students already know about a topic or pose a question that fosters a discussion about previous learning. This is about memory retrieval and works well in a collaborative setting if your students are typically shy or lack confidence. You can even make it competitive by having students recall as much as they can about a topic or as many relevant answers to a proposed question and then have student teams count up the number of unique answers they generated. If you traditionally ask students to do a warm-up in their notebook, consider small changes such as colorful tools like sticky notes or markers and chart paper to increase motivation.

2. Utilize Pictures

Consider giving students a collection of images. Give students time to discuss what they see in the picture. Ask them to sort photos using pre-determined or open-ended categories. Consider using Google Earth as a tool to get students excited about the content in front of them. Allowing students to digitally explore a new place prior to learning content is a great way to hook students.

3. Make Videos Interactive

You are probably already using videos in some fashion. Consider how videos can be used to hook students. Simply showing a video and standing at the back of the room wondering if anyone cares will have a much lower return on the investment of time. Instead, turn down the sound to narrate a specific portion of the video or ask a probing question to assess how the content of the video is resonating with students. Shorter videos will have a more significant impact on students because short videos help us avoid the play-and-pray approach—basically hoping they get it—which does nothing more than increase the chance of students becoming disengaged.

4. Incorporate Costumes, Characters, and Props

I get that this is not for everyone, but imagine your students' faces when you are dressed up in character! There is power in being silly, and certainly dressing up invites laughter and fun into the classroom. If this is not for you, consider using mystery props to invite curiosity and spark conversation, or use a mystery bag and ask students to guess what is inside.

This approach will make a lesson come alive. Whether it is using objects to engage students in a gallery walk or encouraging them to touch and talk about the shared objects, using simple objects creatively offers an opportunity to build excitement and clarify key concepts prior to the main lesson.

5. Preview Key Vocabulary

Previewing vocabulary can be a great way to hook students and ensure that all learners can be successful later in the lesson. A quick game can engage students, but you should avoid playing guessing games to define words; you can lose time quickly getting students to make up possible defi-nitions. Instead, share the words, their definitions, and an example of how the word is used in context. Then engage students in an activity to create mental hooks to the new words.

Allow teams to work together to list synonyms, create a symbol, or draw a team picture to represent the word. Have each team share their ideas. Turn this into a friendly competition. For example, each team shares a picture and votes for the picture that best represents the word. To add interest among peers, teams may only vote for others, not themselves.

The Main Lesson

Once your students are hooked, they will be ready to engage in more demanding content. The bulk of learning occurs during the main body of the lesson. However, this is also the time in which you may notice students "checking out" or becoming disengaged. Many learners, especially those distracted by their mood, emotions, or disingenuous attitude toward the task, need to be intentionally reconnected throughout the lesson (DiNapoli & Miller, 2022).

Researchers found that motivation can change, and each of us falls on a spectrum of willingness to engage in challenging tasks (Szalavitz, 2012). Some students will work hard regardless of perceived difficulty. These students are going to show up ready to learn, but most students will need more than intrinsic motivation to get started. When students are able to work through challenges because they are motivated to do so, your classroom will inevitably remain calm.

Here are four strategies to cultivate calm through cognitive engagement during the lesson:

1. Retrieval and Spacing

Spacing is done in response to the brain's limited ability to absorb information. Cognitive overload happens when the brain is asked to remember too much at once (Talking HealthTech, 2021). Repeatedly revisit concepts and avoid lessons that cram in too much information at once by breaking your lesson into shorter increments. Depending on the age group of your students, space your lesson into 5-, 10-, or 15-minute blocks of time with one or two minutes spent on retrieval.

Retrieval is a strategy to check for understanding while spacing the lesson into smaller increments. Instead of testing students' knowledge at the end of the lesson, retrieval is a one- to two-minute check to clear up any misconceptions and help students with recall. Retrieval is not used to engage students in critical thinking or deep examination of content. Rather, ask students one simple question about the who, what, when, or where related to the content. Most of your "why" questions involve deeper levels of thinking and will come after time is spent on simple recall.

2. Massed Practice Followed by Interleaving

Massed practice is controlled learning in which you teach one skill at a time. Massed practice is often necessary when teaching students a new skill such as decoding short /a/ or solving a mathematical equation.

Massed practice breaks learning into skills, which produces quicker results but may not be effective for long-term learning (Lyle et al., 2022). Think of massed practice as systematic, direct instruction. Then you can help students apply multiple skills they have learned using interleaving, which mixes previous learning with new learning (Sriram, 2020).

Interleaving improves your ability to transfer new skills to unfamiliar situations, after massed practice is introduced (Firth et al., 2021). When learning two or more related concepts or skills, practice both skills during the lesson and mix the types of tasks students are asked to do or vary the design of problems in front of them rather than giving students more of the same over and over again (Firth et al., 2021). Simple examples include finding areas of squares, circles, and rectangles during the same lesson rather than just working with one shape at a time or comparing and contrasting similarities and differences among multiple characters rather than analyzing one at a time. During writing, for example, require students to analyze two approaches to plot development prior to developing their own style.

Another part of constructing knowledge is to revisit past lessons and force the brain to determine which strategy or skill will help with the task at hand. Interleaving invites students to recall an experience in which they solved something before giving them the confidence to do it again (Firth et al., 2021). To build long-term memory, you can add in a few questions from previous lessons on current tests. This develops connections between and across concepts to build a greater depth of understanding.

3. Movement

Consider small ways to get students moving. Movement provides the brain with a boost of dopamine and primes students for deeper learning.

Overall, your lesson should include many activities, strategies, and checks for understanding in order to increase engagement and ultimately cultivate calm.

Optimistic Closure

Optimistic closure is just as important as the first five minutes and the main body of the lesson. However, if you have been teaching for any length of time, you have felt too rushed to close your lesson at times. Think of optimistic closure as a way to extend learning by checking in with students before they leave your classroom, even if you only have one or two minutes to spare at the end of your lesson.

Students' feelings about a lesson's level of engagement transfer to the next lesson (Vasalampi et al., 2021). That is why optimistic closure is more than just about summarizing learning, clearing up misconceptions, and priming students before the next lesson; it is also about human connection. Optimistic closure is about connecting emotion and learning at the end of the lesson because it invites social and emotional engagement into the cognitive process, making learning sticky. Above all, the activities or strategies used to close your lesson should be fun and generate excitement for what is coming tomorrow!

Here are five strategies to cultivate calm through cognitive engagement:

1. Let It Snow

Pose a summary question at the end of the lesson. Even something as simple as "What did you learn today?" or something as specific as a math problem can be used to demonstrate understanding. Give students one to two minutes to record their thinking. Ask them to ball up their response and give them an opportunity to throw their snowball one time. Obviously, it is important to set boundaries to ensure students can have fun while keeping your classroom calm. Ask each student to pick up a snowball and invite a few students to share. If you are concerned students will purposely write inappropriate messages, use a slightly different approach. Instead of snowballs, call them basketballs and allow each student to shoot a basket (into a bucket or trash can) on their way out the door. You can take a look at their responses after class.

2. Act It Out!

Ask teams to create a tableau—a motionless scene—with their bodies to summarize content during the lesson or as a summary after the lesson. For example, students learning about the Revolutionary War may depict a battle scene after studying the Battle of Bunker Hill.

3. Doodle

Ask students to draw a rough sketch to depict their learning. Set a one- to three-minute timer, so they understand the sketch is meant to be a quick summarizer instead of an art contest.

4. Ball Toss

Students quickly share one thing they learned when they catch the ball. Consider how students will need to be positioned around the room. Use a ball that is soft and clarify rules for tossing the ball around the room.

5. Hashtag

Ask students to individually write a hashtag that best matches what they learned. Allow students to share their ideas in a small group and ask each group to select one idea to share with the rest of the class. This gives you instant access to their ideas and offers a quick way to check for any misconceptions.

Cognitive engagement is about students' willingness to invest in their work and engage in a productive struggle. Therefore, it is essential to examine the structure of each lesson and intentionally plan engagement strategies that promote cognition at the beginning, middle, and end of the class. The danger of focusing on cognitive engagement alone is the pressure to "get it all in" and reverting to a sit-and-get lesson structure. This inevitably robs students and teachers of their sense of calm. Instead, plan lessons that are rooted in behavioral, emotional, and social engagement to foster cognitive engagement.

Effort Does Not Always Produce the Desired Result

For your own sense of calm, it is important to note that effort does not always produce desired results. My staff and I had systems in place for engaging families who appeared to be disengaged in school. We were creative with our outreach efforts and had incentives for increasing attendance or completing homework. We held one-on-one meetings, created individual plans, and provided wrap-around services in any way we possibly could to improve student engagement for those who seemed disengaged.

Many times our efforts paid off. Other times our efforts did not produce the results we had hoped for, and it seemed that no matter what we tried, we could not reengage the family or student we so desperately wanted to help. It is important for you to know that when we're talking about engagement, there are times in which you have planned a very engaging lesson and included various strategies for engaging students during all parts of the lesson, and you still may have a student or two who remains disengaged.

As you reflect on this chapter, remember that behavioral, social, emotional, and cognitive engagement strategies work together to cultivate calm. When you are frustrated, remember to be kind to yourself. As we will learn in subsequent chapters, there are many factors that disrupt calm and affect our ability to learn. Continue to examine your practices, but also celebrate your successes often. Without an intentional pause to notice what is working, you may jeopardize the good work you are doing by focusing solely on the negative. As you know, when students are disengaged, it causes an emotional reaction and makes good teachers question themselves. Instead, focus on having more fun with your students by using the strategies suggested in this chapter or incorporating best practices for engagement that you already know. You will feel the shift to a calmer learning culture as a result.

Calm Classrooms Are Born Out of Engaging Lessons

Behavioral, social, emotional, and cognitive engagement cultivate emotional awareness, safety and belonging, and connected relationships so that learning can occur. When we engage students in the curriculum, we need to consider whether we are creating excitement, curiosity, and interest that causes students to want to learn more. Take a moment to ask yourself, "Which dimension of engagement is a strength of mine? Which dimension is least natural for me and why?"

Consider how small changes can make an enormous difference in student engagement. It is a radical idea, but if we make our classrooms both welcoming and highly engaging, we will inevitably create a calmer classroom.

3

Understand Students Who Experience Trauma

I remember at the start of a school year when a 4th grade teacher stopped me in the hallway to ask, "Did the 3rd grade teachers even teach writing last year?" Her tone indicated a load of judgment toward the students and their previous teachers. I looked at her funny. "What do you mean? Of course, they did." I had a collection of student writing portfolios saved in my office. I thought, "I better show her just how much they can do so she can change her attitude quickly." But I decided to listen instead. "They are not even writing complete sentences," she went on to say. This puzzled me. I continued to listen. "It's like we have to go back to the basics. We are teaching 1st and 2nd grade skills." Curious, I asked to see some of her students' work.

Clearly, some of her students demonstrated strong writing skills, but I could not deny there were students who had somehow forgotten everything they knew in June. I was shocked. Their work was not reflective of what I knew they were capable of producing. Many students experience summer slide, but this was more like summer derailment. In the early years of my principalship, it felt like we often took two steps forward and three steps back when meeting the needs of our students.

Desperate for my students to make academic progress, I started to study trauma and memory because I knew many of my students had experienced trauma. The more I learned, the more I wanted to share with staff.

Over time, our staff began to learn about trauma-informed practices and became committed to relationship building and using equitable practices to ensure our students were given access to an education that matched their needs.

In the case of my students, many of their families were from Central America and Mexico and had fled from violence and poverty in their home countries. I knew that many of our young students had not only experienced trauma, but their exposure to trauma was often chronic, repeated, and ongoing and continued long after arriving in the United States.

Despite our best efforts, sometimes it felt like we were starting over every September. This never deterred me from believing in their abilities, and many of my teachers held students to high standards too. We openly talked about ways to avoid learned helplessness. We noticed many students develop a greater sense of belief in themselves. It was not uncommon for a student to share their growth with me or visit their previous teacher to tell them about their progress. We often used the announcements as a vehicle to praise progress. Individual students and whole classes of students cheered when they heard the names of students who demonstrated learning gains on assessments.

We cultivated calm by implementing trauma-informed pedagogy, which primed students to learn. We had data to show that students were learning and they were growing academically from year to year. However, this took time, and in the beginning, many of us felt ill-prepared to support students who had experienced trauma. We had to be willing to learn and grow together if we were going to be serious about supporting our most vulnerable students.

While many teachers and school leaders understand students need help, it is alarming that formal training and teacher preparatory programs have spent very little time on trauma-informed pedagogy in the past. Research shows that teachers report feeling unprepared to support students who have experienced trauma (Dorado et al., 2016).

This feeling of "not knowing" can disrupt our ability to remain calm when students display the symptoms of trauma. We can also feel our sense of calm robbed when the adults around us respond in a way that is not equitable or culturally relevant and we are unsure how to speak up. It is more important than ever to empower teachers with trauma-informed pedagogy and communication tools to proactively and responsibly support students who need us the most.

In some states, there is a lack of universal trauma-informed care models within public education systems (Thomas et al., 2019). Luckily, this is starting to change. As of 2019, 16 states require that teachers receive professional development on trauma-informed care in schools. On a national level, the United States Congress passed the Trauma-Informed Schools Act of 2019. "This bill provides for the use of trauma-informed practices in public elementary and secondary schools and allows states to use certain federal funds to train teachers in such practices" (115th Congress, 2018).

Traditionally, students experiencing trauma have been sent to the school counselor or an administrator (Rahimi et al., 2021). Most schools are not staffed with enough counselors to address the increasing number of students facing adverse childhood experiences (ASCA, 2019). Teachers deserve to have access to this information and the opportunity to develop the know-how to support students, both proactively and in response to the needs of students suffering from traumatic stress.

Empowering teachers with knowledge about how stress impacts brain development and school performance is necessary if we are going to support our most vulnerable students (Pechtel & Pizzagalli, 2011).

Simply put, implementing trauma-informed practices requires a shared understanding among all staff of the types of evidence-based approaches that promote empathy and communication to ensure individual student needs are met. While we need to understand the neurological, psychological, and social effects of trauma, with the right interventions, students who have experienced trauma are fully capable of learning and should be held to high standards. In order to cultivate a calmer classroom, it is important to develop our knowledge base in order to implement trauma-informed practices.

Over half of high-risk children and youth are not getting adequate professional help, and only 38 percent of public schools provide treatment to students who need therapeutic support (Office of Justice Programs, 2020). "While individual treatment and clinical methods were long seen as the most effective approach to addressing trauma and posttraumatic stress disorder" (Thomas et al., 2019, para. 5), trauma-informed care in schools is a promising approach to providing healing support to our most vulnerable youth. It is easy to understand that if students feel safe, known, and cared for within their schools, they are more likely to learn to their full potential (Aupperle et al., 2012). Most important, the types of interventions we apply to support students who have experienced trauma must be research-based, effective, easy to apply, and universal in order for our schools to be places of healing.

Calmer classrooms are cultivated when adults

- Build a knowledge base of trauma-informed pedagogy.
- Create a culture of safety.
- Improve communication to boost empathetic responses.
- Examine personal history and social identity.

Throughout this chapter, we will build a knowledge base of trauma-informed pedagogy, discuss ways to design a trauma-sensitive classroom, learn ways to improve communication to boost empathy, and recognize the impact of vicarious trauma, all to cultivate a calmer classroom.

Build a Knowledge Base of Trauma-Informed Pedagogy

Note: Before we dig further into this topic, it is important to remember that all states designate school staff to be mandated reporters. By law, we are responsible to report reasonable suspicions of abuse or neglect. Please ensure that you are familiar with and confident in your role as a mandated reporter.

Trauma is possibly the largest public health issue facing our children today (CDC, 2019). Therefore, we need to understand how to support our students who have or are currently experiencing trauma. Working with students who have experienced trauma is not easy. The type of behavior that may manifest has the potential to disrupt calm. It is not just about feeling a loss of calm while a behavior is occurring; there are potentially long-lasting effects of disruptive behavior that can shake both teachers and other students. In order to remain calm, we must begin by building an awareness of the various types of trauma students may have experienced or are continually experiencing and apply effective strategies to support and nurture students. Trauma-informed pedagogy is critically important to understand because, without this understanding, we could feel out of control in our own classrooms and become overridden with fear about when the next unwanted behavior will occur.

Being aware of how trauma impacts learning can empower educators to utilize strategies to build a trauma-sensitive classroom.

To begin with, let's explore some important definitions:

- Trauma-sensitive vs. trauma-informed
- Adverse childhood experiences
- Psychological trauma
- Acute trauma, chronic trauma, and complex trauma
- Collective identity trauma
- Manifestation of trauma
- Vicarious trauma

Trauma-Sensitive Versus Trauma-Informed

There are some nuanced differences between being trauma-sensitive and trauma-informed. A *trauma-sensitive* school or classroom is about creating an environment of safety and support. In order to achieve this, the adults in the building work as a team to share in the responsibility of making school a place in which relationships are prioritized and *all* students can be successful (Trauma-Sensitive Schools, 2022).

The term *trauma-informed* is often used in the behavioral health field and refers to the behavioral health services offered in a school through coordinated delivery and responsive care (SAMHSA, n.d.). This includes having social workers or mental health therapists assigned directly to schools, access to healthcare at school, or support with economic challenges such as food insecurity.

While many of us have experiences working in schools that lack the necessary services needed to be fully trauma-informed, we can all create a trauma-sensitive culture through our interactions, beliefs, and willingness to create structures and processes that support students who have been victimized. Later in this chapter we will examine practices that create these positive conditions that will benefit all students.

Adverse Childhood Experiences

Adverse Childhood Experiences (ACEs) are events that occur in childhood (0–17 years) that have the potential to be traumatic. ACEs can include physical and emotional abuse, neglect, caregiver mental illness, and household violence. Additionally, a child's environment can disrupt their "sense of safety, stability, and bonding" (CDC, 2017). Exposure to substance abuse, mental health problems, or incarceration of a parent are also reported ACEs. This is certainly not an exhaustive list. ACEs are linked to chronic health problems, mental illness, and substance use problems later in life (CDC, 2017).

Regardless of where children are born, their socioeconomic status, or housing situation, many children experience childhood trauma. In fact, almost two-thirds of adults have reported experiencing a traumatic event during childhood (Anda et al., 2006). Shockingly, 46 percent of all U.S. children have experienced at least one ACE before their eighth birthday, and more than 20 percent have experienced two or more. Compounding ACEs—that is, having experienced three or more adverse experiences as a child—can lead to a greater risk of health problems, including anxiety, depression, and suicide (Velemínský et al., 2020).

ACEs increase the risk of developing severe emotional and behavioral problems (Offerman et al., 2022). There are also long-term effects on health and well-being due to high levels of toxic stress that occur as a result of ACEs (RWJF, 2021). Long-term risk for "smoking, alcoholism, depression, heart and liver diseases, and dozens of other illnesses and unhealthy behaviors" have also been reported as consequences of ACEs, with 33 percent of children with two or more ACEs ending up with a special health care need "compared to 13.6 percent of children without ACEs" (RWJF, 2021).

Some children are at an even greater risk, including several racial/ ethnic minority groups that we will discuss when we explore collective identity trauma.

Psychological Trauma

When we experience a threatening event (i.e., something that puts our life in danger, either real or perceived), our nervous system reacts by entering survival mode. The amygdala, found in the lower part of the brain, sends signals to the brain to motivate us to fight, protect ourselves, or flee to escape (Araminta, 2020b). When children experience abuse at home, a freeze—or stay-put—response is most likely activated because there is no option to fight back or flee, causing them to become "stuck" in an emotional and psychological shutdown to prevent the psyche from becoming too overwhelmed. This can cause the nervous system to mistake safe environments and safe people as threats because the nervous system remains frozen in a state of arousal (Araminta, 2020b).

Psychological trauma occurs when harmful experiences or events create chronic stress and affect overall well-being, which in-turn can disrupt brain development, making learning and retention difficult (SAMHSA, n.d.). Memory, comprehension, organizational skills, and the ability to regulate emotions are all effects of childhood trauma (Wolpow et al., 2009), which makes learning more difficult.

Acute Trauma, Chronic Trauma, and Complex Trauma

Acute trauma results from a single incident that causes our autonomic nervous system (ANS) to become stuck in a threat response (Bryant, 2019). The ANS threat response is meant to protect us and help signal that we are in danger. When a threat is over, the autonomic nervous system's job is to return to a normal, regulated state. However, if a threat is so overwhelming that the ANS is unable to return to a regulated state, it will inform the brain that a threat is still present (Araminta, 2020a). When this happens, the event has caused a traumatic response in the body. Examples of this type of traumatic experience include exposure to death or being threatened with death, serious injury, or sexual violation. When symptoms such as negative mood, avoidance, or arousal last for at least three days after the event, this stress response is often diagnosed as a traumatic response to a signal event (2019). Acute trauma has the potential to cause long-term symptoms, depending on the severity of the single event.

Chronic trauma is repeated and prolonged, such as ongoing domestic violence or abuse. Due to the severity of this type of trauma, professional help is often necessary to help children (and adults) heal. Unlike acute trauma, which is caused by one single event, these events happen multiple times and can take years to surface, whereas acute trauma generally shows up in a matter of weeks (Araminta, 2020b). Examples include prolonged child abuse, repeated sexual abuse, or ongoing exposure to domestic violence. This type of trauma can lead to avoidant behavior, social withdrawal, anxiety, depression, anger, or violent outbursts. It would not be uncommon for victims of chronic trauma to overreact to normal events or have low self-worth.

Similar to chronic trauma, *complex trauma* is exposure to varied and multiple events that occur over a period of time, generally within domestic or intimate relationships. Repeated domestic violence or abuse leaves a victim feeling trapped (Courtois, 2004). This type of trauma is even more complicated when experienced by a child who is psychologically and physically unable to make sense of how a caregiver, who is supposed to be safe and protective, is causing such harm.

Trauma expert Bessel van der Kolk (2015) describes how long-term trauma exposure literally becomes trapped in the body and the brain rewires itself. When a threat occurs, the parasympathetic nervous system's (PNS) job is to return us to a state of inner calm. The PNS allows us to return to normal cognitive functioning, and while we may still feel a little upset or elevated, we are able to begin the process of regulating. For children living with trauma, the limbic system stays in a heightened state at all times, which causes a child to experience the feeling of constantly being in survival mode or on edge. The brain and body remain in high alert, which can make it difficult to form positive relationships. Thoughts of overwhelm can become a new normal (Ada, 2019).

Over time the body will even begin to produce somatic symptoms, such as chronic headaches and stomachaches because the body's response to long-term trauma exposure changes the functionality of the immune system, causing a range of chronic health conditions (van der Kolk, 2015). Appropriate treatment for complex trauma can vary in intensity and duration depending on the needs of the victim. In the beginning, treatment is focused on establishing safety and a focus on self-regulation skills (Courtois, 2004).

There are research-based strategies to support students who are experiencing trauma that can be applied in any classroom. While a teacher cannot be held responsible to "fix" the symptoms of childhood trauma, a classroom rooted in trauma-responsive practices can make a positive difference in a child's life. A consistent relationship with a trusted teacher offers a child an opportunity to learn in a safe environment, which is necessary to ensure students are not retraumatized at school. We will explore practical strategies that can support students experiencing various forms of trauma, which can complement clinical treatment.

Collective Identity Trauma

Individual trauma is a traumatic event that happens to a person, whereas *collective trauma* occurs when members of a group feel they have been subjected to a traumatic event, series of events, or history that has left a lasting impact on members of the group. The term *collective trauma* is also known as community-wide trauma, racial or cultural trauma, historical trauma, intergenerational trauma, mass trauma, and multigenerational trauma.

Most of us remember where we were on September 11, 2001, when two planes crashed into the World Trade Center. As the evil actions continued and the horrific replay of events was shown over and over again, many of us bonded together in support of our country. Flags were hung, communities came together to support one another, and a collective strength surfaced among strangers who had one thing in common: unity for our country. Most of us felt a sense of unity.

During this season of my life, I was a 4th grade classroom teacher in a diverse part of Maryland. Two of the women I worked with were Muslim. As most Americans felt a sense of unity after 9/11, both of my Muslim friends described quite a different experience. The outright discrimination they each experienced after these devastating events made it difficult for both of them to cope, not only due to how they were treated but also because they grieved for their country just as much as their non-Muslim neighbors. Discrimination can lead to cascading trauma, which is the impact of cumulative exposure to lifetime adversity. Both of my friends reported an ongoing struggle to feel that they belonged even though they also lived here and their religious beliefs were polar opposite to the extreme terrorists that had caused horrific harm.

Discrimination is a form of trauma that seems to have ambiguous endpoints, which can compound feelings of not knowing how bad things will get or when true recovery can happen. Watching news coverage repeatedly can intensify these feelings.

For example, brutal killings of unarmed Black people put a spotlight on systemic racism in the United States. Repeated exposure to this level of targeted violence can have mental health consequences for Black people who continuously witness or experience racial catastrophes.

As Black, Latinx, and Indigenous communities in the United States suffered disproportionately from COVID-19, compounded historical trauma, systemic racism, and persistent poverty led to a deeper cascade of collective trauma (Silver et al., 2021). Furthermore, some healthcare workers who were already vulnerable from exposure to trauma prior to the pandemic reported that their mental health worsened during the pandemic, which has now been named a collective traumatic experience (American Psychological Association, 2021).

Natural disasters are another example of collective identity trauma, commonly referred to as *community-related trauma*. Natural disasters can cause a psychological impact on all who experience it. Episodes of anxiety, mood swings, attention problems, and even flashbacks are all common reactions after a disaster.

Another type of collective trauma is known as *generational trauma*, intergenerational trauma, or transgenerational trauma. This is trauma that is passed down through generations of family members. Generational trauma was first spotlighted after reports of high rates of stress, anxiety, and depression among children whose caregivers had survived the Holocaust (Rakoff, 1966). Many of these children were experiencing symptoms such as low self-esteem, nightmares, anxiety, and guilt (Feldman & Rottman, 2018). Children have the potential to experience stress when parents or caregivers are emotionally unavailable due to the feeling of always being on guard or reliving horrible experiences.

While anyone can be affected by generational trauma, populations who have been exposed to prolonged exposure to poverty, racism, catastrophic events, war, and abuse are most at risk. Furthermore, students living in disadvantaged environments, including unstable family structures or harsh parenting, are at a higher risk for physical and psychological illnesses (Mitchell et al., 2014). Generational trauma can affect the immune system and make it overactive or underactive, putting people affected by generational trauma at a greater risk for illnesses (Gillespie, 2020).

We can look to research about our DNA to help us understand how trauma is passed from generation to generation. Imagine that the cap at the end of your shoelace, which holds the shoelace intact, is similar to the protective cap found at the end of every strand of DNA. These caps are known as *telomeres*. As we age, our telomeres become shorter and shorter. When we are under stress, our telomeres become shorter and shorter. "Shorter telomeres cause our DNA to become unstable and prone to express disease," and multiple studies show that shorter telomeres are a "cellular marker for psychosocial stress" (Kim et al., 2017). From this research we know that shortened telomeres among children are correlated with trauma exposure (Mitchell et al., 2014). In particular, when compared to children from advantaged environments, children from disadvantaged environments are born with shorter telomeres, giving us insight as to how trauma seeps into our DNA.

However, this research provides promising news. A Nobel prize was given to researchers who discovered that telomeres can regrow (Nobel Media, 2019). We know from science and research that families who receive support in learning how to foster an enriching, supportive home environment can help reverse the negative effects of trauma (Feldman & Rottman, 2018). One way we can regrow telomeres is through stress management. For children, this means when they learn to regulate emotions and manage stress, they build resilience skills. The power of human connection cannot be underestimated. The most effective way for students to learn to manage stress responses is through a consistent relationship with an adult.

Manifestation of Trauma

Whether students are exposed to one traumatic event, chronic/frequent events, or complex/multiple traumatic events, the body responds by activating a fight, flight, or freeze response. These events are processed by the amygdala, a central component of the brain's fear detection and anxiety circuits. Even if a child is unsure of what is happening around them or unable to make sense of a situation, the body is having a physical response and stress chemicals are released (Kim et al., 2017). As a result, cortisol levels become elevated, and signals of harm are sent through various parts of the brain, causing the sympathetic nervous system to activate (Perlman & Pelphrey, 2011). This causes an increase in heart rate, metabolic rate, blood pressure, and overall stress hormones. This chain reaction has a deep impact on brain development. The National Child Traumatic Stress Network (NCTSN) (n.d.) outlines the manifestations of trauma that may be present in students as a result of exposure to ACES by various ages.

Preschool children may demonstrate manifestations of trauma by crying, screaming, whimpering, and trembling. You may also notice children at this age experiencing fear of being separated from their parent/caregiver; they may eat poorly or lose weight or have nightmares. This is not an exhaustive list.

Elementary school children, ages 6–12 years old, might begin to isolate themselves more often. Students in this age group might become irritable or disruptive or have outbursts of behavior. They might start fights very easily and become dysregulated quickly. You may also notice students becoming more anxious or have a hard time concentrating.

Middle and high school children may become very unmotivated to complete schoolwork. During the adolescent and young adult period we can see a lot of mood swings happening as a response to trauma, including acting-out behaviors such as reckless driving, engaging in high-risk behaviors, oppositional defiant disorder, and academic difficulties. In some cases, students develop eating disorders or show an increase in promiscuous behavior.

When traumatized students have difficulty with self-regulation, demonstrate negative thinking, and have a hard time trusting adults, this type of behavior often leads to labeling students as rude or disrespectful. These students often haven't learned to express emotions in a healthy way, and their behavior manifests as aggression, avoidance, shutting down, or other unfavorable behaviors. These are some of the behaviors that begin to rob us of our calm.

These behaviors are challenging for us as adults because our amygdala is firing off, and our sense of safety may be harmed or threatened because we are exposed to this unfavorable behavior. It is uncomfortable and emotionally painful.

When we think about working with students who have experienced trauma, we have to remember that their behavior is not personal. Lacking positive attachments in childhood leads to an underdeveloped sense of attunement, making it hard for students to understand the effects of their behavior.

Coupled with our body's response to the manifestation of unfavorable behaviors is the fact that we care about our students. There is a cost of caring. In the next section we will discuss vicarious trauma as it relates to the cost of caring.

Vicarious Trauma

Vicarious trauma is also known as secondary traumatic stress (STS), compassion fatigue (CF), and critical incident stress (CIS) (Branson, 2019). Educators can experience vicarious trauma as a form of work-related trauma due to exposure to the traumatic experiences of students or by witnessing unfavorable behaviors in the classroom that manifest as a result of trauma. Each person's experience is unique, and vicarious trauma can lead to burnout and cause a fearful inner response, but it can also cause an educator to approach students with a deeper sense of empathy. It is important to understand that responses to vicarious trauma can be negative, positive, or neutral (Bell et al., 2003).

A neutral response is not meant to diminish the character or care of a teacher, but it rather speaks to the educator's level of resilience (Love & Langley, 2020). Simply put, having the tools and resources to manage the potential effects of vicarious trauma empowers educators to help their students without ending up in a state of burnout.

Applying strategies to manage the risks associated with vicarious trauma can lead to positive effects as well. A step further from a neutral response is the ability to have an internal positive response to vicarious trauma. This is known as *vicarious resilience*. In this way, public servants, such as educators, may be able to draw inspiration from students who demonstrate emotional resilience in the face of experiencing trauma.

Furthermore, vicarious resilience is about building deeper empathy toward victims. Educators may find deeper meaning in their work by understanding that building a positive and consistent relationship with a student releases oxytocin, giving the student a sense of hope through connection with their teacher (Tereshchenko & Smolnikova, 2019). Oxytocin is a hormone of trust, and when a student develops that feeling through a relationship with an educator, this can make all the difference in the world to a student's ability to heal. Oxytocin is produced through social connections from infancy on, but if a child does not experience this level of attachment during their early years, they will have a more difficult time with behavior regulation.

Educators are in a unique position to build connected relationships with students who may not have experienced the feeling of positive attachment at home. That is why it is essential for educators to be well cared for to begin with, creating a stronger likelihood that they will have the skills to manage the impact of vicarious trauma.

Educators who have experienced a high number of ACEs themselves may be at higher risk for experiencing the symptoms of vicarious trauma. We can overcome a negative response to vicarious trauma by receiving our own support so that we can best support students. This includes social connection at work, preparation and training to understand the manifestation of difficult behavior and what to do about it, and a supportive process for discussing traumatic responses like outbursts and aggression in the classroom. Thus, teachers need support in order to support their students.

Chapter 5 is devoted to sharing research-based strategies, tools, and tips to develop a neutral or positive response to vicarious trauma for the purpose of educator well-being and retention.

What Can Be Done?

To begin with, creating a trauma-sensitive classroom is good for all children regardless of their exposure to trauma. It's important to be aware of the potential to further stigmatize students who already feel isolated or different. If a child's trauma history is not handled with the appropriate level of care, students can be left to feel shame after disclosing intimate details of their experiences. Of course, we have an obligation to report reasonable suspicions of child abuse or neglect, but it is not necessary to have a full report about a student's traumatic experience in order to be supportive (Trauma-Sensitive Schools, 2022).

We know that traumatic experiences can have significant effects on the student learning process but that these effects are not necessarily permanent. Severity may depend on the approaches taken by teaching staff—consciously or not.

We can better understand the use of practices that support and promote the well-being of our students. The success of our students is determined not only by graduation but also by how we equip them to reach their full potential and thrive. This work requires all adults to make a commitment to creating trauma-sensitive classrooms and schools.

In order to cultivate a calmer classroom, it is critical that we think about how to manage students' emotions rather than fix or deny them. To do this, we as adults need to understand how to manage our own emotions when working with students who have experienced trauma. Every time an unfavorable behavior occurs, we risk losing our sense of calm. This is an ongoing process.

Calm is practiced. When I felt angry when students were aggressive, aggressive behavior was a trigger for me. Witnessing it made me feel very unsafe. If a student throws something across the room or flips a table, it is only natural to lose our sense of calm.

I have witnessed this type of behavior more times than I care to remember. While it was not always easy, I had to practice staying regulated in those moments. I did not do this perfectly, and believe me, there were times I struggled to remain calm in a crisis. However, with practice, each of us can get stronger.

Create a Culture of Safety

As humans, our ability to maintain supportive relationships has always been crucial to our survival. Children especially have a great desire to be welcomed into a group. A classroom community provides an opportunity for children to feel that they belong.

Indeed, children who have experienced trauma may disrupt class instruction, which can cause us to lose our sense of calm. It is not unusual for a student to have a difficult time trusting adults and peers, especially those in positions of power, when they have experienced fractured relationships in the past. In this section, we will discuss how to thoughtfully design a trauma-sensitive classroom with simple strategies to cultivate a calmer classroom.

Excellent behavior management begins with the teacher. A good start is to understand yourself and your emotions. A teacher's ability to remain calm and patient while evoking optimism and confidence is essential (Akhtar & Saleem, 2020).

The mood of an educator can have significant influence on how students behave. When your energy reflects tension, frustration, or annoyance, this leads to a tension-filled classroom where students are more likely to misbehave.

The good news is that cultivating calm using trauma-sensitive approaches is not super complicated. Here are some intentional trauma-sensitive strategies to cultivate a calmer classroom:

1. Decide

You decide to remain calm throughout your day before your students arrive. Each day before the morning bell, set aside some time to sit quietly at your desk. Relax in your chair by taking a few deep breaths.

Decide that no matter what occurs that day, you will choose calm. This technique, used by many professional athletes, appears almost too simple. Nevertheless, it is astonishing how a simple choice can make a huge difference.

2. Slow Down

Slowing down your movements will also slow down your mind, making you less distracted and more intentional in your responses toward students. Racing mindlessly from one task to the next, as many teachers are prone to do, causes us to easily lose our calm when something unexpected happens.

3. Speak Softly

Speaking calmly when giving directions, providing information, and responding to your students is an easy way to create a safe environment.

4. Normalize Breathing

It is incredible what a few long, slow breaths can do for adults and students. Almost immediately, your blood pressure drops, your face softens, and the tension in your body dissipates. Take a couple of deep breaths every hour to expel the anticipation and excitement from your classroom. Set a timer to remind yourself to breathe, and invite your students to breathe with you.

Oxygen provides vital energy and mental capacity. Furthermore, by becoming aware of your breathing, you will not only calm your own nerves, sharpen your mental acuity, and brighten your mood, but you will also become a calming, centering influence on your students.

Improve Communication to Boost Empathetic Responses

In general, a positive relationship with a trusted adult can change everything for a child who faces vulnerable circumstances. Simply put, a positive social environment during childhood greatly impacts a child's ability to cope. It's not what you do; it's how you are. Essentially, attitude is everything. The respect students develop for their teacher has a lot to do with disposition, presence, charisma, and empathetic responses. These cultivate a calmer classroom. Emotional *affect* is something we can continue to develop.

Here are intentional strategies that improve communication to boost empathetic responses:

1. Red Hearts

Have you ever been in a situation where an adult made a difficult student situation worse? We all have. I remember one incident in my career that changed how we operated as a school. One of our students was in and out of the foster care system. We had been working on self-regulation with her for a long time. Luckily, she had an excellent relationship with her teacher. Still, it was hard for her to regulate her emotions; some days were better than others. One morning she came to school after her third foster family had rejected her. She was fragile, vulnerable, and deregulated.

One particular morning she ordered chicken nuggets for lunch. You might work in a school like mine in which lunches are ordered centrally so children cannot change their order. By the time lunch came, this student wanted pizza instead of chicken nuggets. She politely asked a cafeteria staff member if she could have pizza instead of chicken nuggets, and the staff member said, "No," and reminded her that students are not allowed to change their lunch choices. The young girl started to become unraveled. At that moment, she was mindful and decided to elicit the help of her teacher rather than letting her emotions get the best of her. Her teacher told her not to worry, and together they would ensure that she got the pizza she wanted. When the teacher went down to the cafeteria, she approached the staff member and said, "I need your help. Please give her pizza today." The teacher received the same response: "No, she ordered chicken nuggets and cannot change her mind." Be aware that this situation is not about giving students what they want all the time. This was about control for this student. With her world spiraling out of control, she needed to have control over something, and on this day it was her lunch choice.

When she was denied again, the student had a complete meltdown. The teacher, feeling helpless, came running to my office to get me. After she explained what was happening, I marched down to that cafeteria as fast as I could get myself there. I looked the staff member directly in the eyes and said, "Give her the pizza," in a loud and aggressive voice. I had clearly lost my calm.

It took a very long time to regulate this student again and convince her that it was OK to eat the slice of pizza. We probably spent a good 90 minutes helping the student return to a state of calm.

That evening I began to wonder what I was doing wrong. I started to think about my role as the leader in this situation. I was so upset that the situation became out of control and that this vulnerable student went into crisis mode when this could have been prevented. I started to think about the actions of the staff member and how rigid she was in that situation.

I began to ask myself, "What messages have I been sending about how we treat students who have experienced trauma? Have you even talked about this enough? Was the staff member actually in the wrong or just doing her job?" I knew I had to help all staff members understand our most vulnerable students. It took me several days to reflect on the situation before I realized we needed a communication tool to help staff understand when a student required intentional care.

I decided to buy every single staff member a red heart sticker that they could place on their badge. Then I went around and taught everyone what the sticker meant, including bus drivers, cafeteria workers, paraeducators, secretaries, building service workers, and anyone who came in contact with our students.

Red heart students need extra patience, compassion, support, and kindness. These kids have histories that tug at our heartstrings. We do everything we can to make sure they are successful.

My job was to help our staff understand when it is appropriate to handle a situation with care and why we might need to bend the rules sometimes to avoid a crisis or help us determine which battles to pick and when to let go. As a result, we began to use the red heart to communicate with one another. Discreetly pointing to the sticker communicated to the other adult in the room, "Stand down," or, "Help me de-escalate the situation." Essentially, this communication tool changed how adults supported one another.

Implementing the red hearts was one of the most significant changes to our culture, and it cost nearly nothing. It was simply a communication tool that we utilized to talk between and among each other, using this as a signal to remind us to take a deep breath and to be gentle during a situation that has the potential to escalate. It also helped us identify students who would need or benefit from mentors.

Students are not aware that they are red hearts. This strategy is used to improve communication among adults and maintain a calmer culture by building empathy. The red heart strategy is intended to support a "handle with care" mindset rather than sharing confidential information about students.

2. Staff-to-Student Mentors

Mentors provide a promising adult relationship for red heart students. Consider who could serve as a mentor for your red heart students. A mentor can become that student's "person." You may ask the mentor to "check in" before the start of the day and "check out" at the end of the day. This is particularly helpful if your red heart student has a contract. We will discuss contracts in depth in Chapter 4.

3. Alert Substitutes to the Red Hearts in Your Class

I realized all of our efforts could be unraveled quickly if substitutes were not aware of how to best support red heart students. This simple form in Figure 3.1 can be a part of your substitute folder. Its purpose is to provide your substitute with best practices to apply when working with a red heart student in your absences. My former counselor wrote this beautiful poem, which sets the tone for communicating with substitutes.

Examine Personal History and Social Identity

In order to manage the symptoms of vicarious trauma, we have to examine our own history and social identity. Thus, we must understand the correlation between our personal background and our ability to manage the potential stress of working with students in trauma.

Our social identity includes our personal values and our identity, including gender, socioeconomic status, race, and other forms of identity that influence how we think and respond to society and our students. This is important for several reasons. First, we need to examine our biases and

FIGURE 3.1
Red Heart Students Communication Tool

Who are Red Heart students at Sunshine School?

They are students who need extra patience, compassion, support, and kindness. These kids have histories that tug at our heartstrings. We do everything we can to make sure they are successful.

Welcome to _____'s classroom.

Student name: _____

"POEM"
by Erin Coco

I am just a kid.
A kid who has a story... please give me compassion.
Sometimes I have a hard time... know that I need your love.
I may need extra patience... remember I am doing my best.
I am part of the Blue Ridge family... and Blue Ridge is my home.

Here's what you should know about me:

_____

_____

_____

Note: *It is not necessary to share a child's entire story or even any of the details. Confidential information should not be shared. Rather, consider sharing best practices such as "Sometimes math feels really hard. I tend to get upset if I feel left out."*

If I'm having a hard time...

_____

_____

_____

Note: *This may include examples such as "Allow me to sit in the calming corner. Allow me to visit my mentor, Ms. Sunshine. Her classroom is Room B."*

Source: The Calmer Network, www.calmerschools.com/resources.

how they show up when working with students and families. Second, we need to examine our beliefs and how they guide our interactions. Third, we need to consider how our own trauma histories may show up and impact how we respond to students. Finally, we need to recognize our readiness to manage the impact of vicarious trauma.

In this section, I will share my own story and social identity. I will reflect on how these aspects of me affect my ability to manage stress. I will invite you to pause and think about your own story and how your history impacts your response to students and families experiencing trauma.

I believe my personal history has had a direct impact on my ability to empathize with students. I was born in 1976 and appeared to be healthy despite a noticeable ear deformity, which affected the shape of my right ear. A few months after I was born, I became very sick. There is a scene in the 1973 movie *The Exorcist* where Regan projectile vomits at Father Karras. That scene can be used to articulate how my body would react to formula. My parents tried every type of formula imaginable, but I continued to vomit after every feeding. This puzzled doctors until one genius made the connection between my ear deformity and potential kidney damage because our ears and kidneys run on the same chromosome. Using a sonogram, they discovered that my left kidney was underdeveloped. My childhood was plagued with painful kidney infections. When I was 11, the kidney was finally removed and I have lived just fine with one kidney for all of these years. This was difficult but not traumatic for me. I was surrounded by caring parents and felt loved.

As an adult, I developed debilitating vertigo that lasted for seven years on and off. Episodes of vertigo were awful, causing me to throw up and making it impossible to move until the dizziness subsided. Today, I have complete hearing loss in my right ear. While these circumstances could be traumatic for anyone, for me, I would classify them as difficult circumstances but not traumatic.

On my 31st birthday, I was diagnosed with a rare and aggressive form of cancer, Merkel cell carcinoma. The cancer formed a tumor on my left cheek. After consulting with a team of doctors, I began treatment immediately. As a result, I underwent several aggressive facial surgeries to remove the tumor, tissues, and test lymph nodes. Additionally, I had extensive rounds of radiation to my face. The cancer damaged the entire left side of my face, and I endured several reconstructive surgeries. Facing cancer was stressful, painful, overwhelming, and scary. While these circumstances could be traumatic for anyone, for me, this was difficult but not traumatic.

However, when I was 16 years old, I was dating a boy much older than me. My 16-year-old self thought it was cool that he liked me until I learned he was cheating on me. Disappointed, I knew I had to be courageous and speak up. On the night I went to break up with him, he sexually assaulted me. I was shocked. I was confused. I was fearful, to say the least. This event and the long-term effects were traumatic for me. Thankfully, with the support of my parents and an incredible therapist, I have been able to heal from the event, but it is something that will be with me forever.

Not all stressful events or difficult circumstances are traumatic. What is traumatic for one person may not be traumatic for another. That is why it is critical to understand this from an individual perspective.

As I reflect on the chronic health issues I have endured, I often ask myself how I made it through so many stressful situations. I am grateful for amazing doctors and modern medicine. In each difficulty, I was met with an incredible amount of support, love, and unity, and as a result experienced personal victory in spite of difficulties. Being connected to people who cared for me empowered me to persevere while enduring a lot of stress. I believe these experiences left me feeling inspired to want to help. I desired to make a difference in my students' lives.

Having the advantage of money, support, medical care, love, consistency, and belonging created a spirit of generosity when working with my students. However, my social identity caused me to be ineffective at times. I easily developed a "white savior" mentality, believing that I could fix my students and save them from harm, as if it were my job to fix them. My intentions were pure but also immature. I did not realize how the privilege I had was affecting how I served students and families. I thought I was doing them a favor by helping them. What I failed to recognize was that my way of helping was not what they always wanted or needed. Over time, I became frustrated when my "help" did not result in a change in the families I was serving. Subconsciously I expected something in return; that is, I wanted to experience a positive result based on my help. I believed they should "get it" because I was doing so much for them. My view was narrow, and my approach was based on my own identity and cultural norms.

Here are intentional strategies to help you understand how your history and social identity show up when working with students who experience trauma:

1. Examine Your History

Take time to reflect on your own story. Ask yourself the following:

- Which parts of my childhood affected me both positively and negatively?
- How did I cope with difficulties or traumatic experiences?
- Who hurt me? Is this similar to the type of hurt my students' experience?
- How did I heal? When do I feel whole?
- In which parts of my life am I still hurting?
- How does my history show up at school?

2. Understand Your Positionality

I chose to dig deeper to understand my biases and how they affected my approach when working with students and families. I am still growing. However, now I know two things for sure: (1) I don't always know what is best. (2) Listening is more important than speaking.

We all have good intentions, and we want to help. Sometimes we burn ourselves out trying to be heroes. Instead, we need to embrace the fact that we do not need to fix children or their caregivers. What they need is for us to listen. We cannot eradicate abuse or neglect (although we must report suspicions of it). We cannot control everything that happens to our students. Instead, we can help them manage symptoms of stress. We can remember that it is not what we *do* for students; it is how we are *with* them.

Simply put, it is our responsibility to remain whole for our students so we can provide a calm environment. We cannot do this if we carry their problems home or remain in a state of judgment toward them or their caregivers. If we operate with the mindset that we must fix or change students, we are going to fail, and it is a disrespectful approach anyway. The gift we can give students is to develop a stable response to their needs and provide them with a calmer classroom in which they feel safe. If we carry their burdens, we will burn out. If we focus on "righting" all of the "wrongs" in the world, we risk becoming righteous. Instead, we can emphasize and connect with our students without placing our views or judgments on them or their families.

Consider this exercise to understand your positionality:

- Identify aspects of your background that have shaped you, including race, religion, socioeconomic status, sexuality, disability status, age, and culture. This is not an exhaustive list.
- How is your background similar to or different from your students?
- How is your "power" as a teacher reflected in your interactions with students and families?
- Identify areas of bias and assumption.
- Consider how you will adequately challenge biases and assumptions.

Calmness on the inside does not imply a lack of passion on the outside (Linsin, 2022). Understanding childhood trauma can help us remain calm because then we come to understand the importance of student relationships and psychological safety in the classroom. We must realize that our ability to cultivate a calmer classroom starts within. This is just as much a personal journey as it is a professional one. If we are going to create a calmer classroom, we need to develop empathy toward our students—even when it is tough—and reflect on practices that are working along with those that need to be upgraded.

In the next chapter, we will continue to examine best practices for classroom management and repairing harm while remaining calm. Our focus on empathy with accountability will provide you with tools for setting boundaries, issuing consequences, and teaching appropriate behaviors without losing your cool.

4

Empathy with Accountability

To cultivate a calmer classroom, it is important to investigate the correlation between student behavior and teacher stress levels. Student behavior is one of the biggest causes of stress among educators (Harmsen et al., 2018). Negative student behavior cultivates discontent for many educators, causing them to seek accountability when students do not meet the expectations for behavior. While it is important for students to be held accountable for their actions, accountability is defined differently from school to school and classroom to classroom. Thus, the topic of having empathy for students while also holding them accountable to learn skills for regulating their behavior is one of great urgency. This chapter will focus on understanding the importance of balancing empathy with accountability in order to foster a calmer classroom.

Researchers from Duke University studied the impact of the COVID-19 pandemic on the development of emotional awareness skills, particularly among students who were socially isolated for a long period of time (Rosanbalm, 2021). They found significantly weakened activity in the "thinking" parts of the brain among students who experienced isolation. Thus, the parts of the brain that manage concentration, decision making, impulse control, and empathy showed decreased competencies (Brendtro, 2015). Isolation leads to pronounced or prolonged stress, which can lead to feelings of emotional distress, fatigue, and disengagement (Rosanbalm,

2021). Although this stress response has the potential to impact learning for all students, those from homes with higher stress or instability are at the greatest risk (Rosanbalm, 2021). It was predicted that schools would see growing achievement gaps, particularly based on socioeconomic status, in the months and years following the pandemic, and it is no surprise these predictions were right.

Over time, a dysregulated stress response system causes neurochemical reactions, which can be toxic to the developing brain. These changes in brain structure and function can cause long-term impairments in memory, attention, mood, decision making, and impulse control (Shonkoff & Garner, 2012). For children and adolescents, these neurobiological changes can, predictably, interfere with school achievement (McLaughlin et al., 2013). There continues to be an urgency to teach students how to calm their stress response system in order to engage the brain.

To be clear, accountability is not about imposing harsh consequences on students, but it is also not about throwing all consequences out the window in an attempt to show empathy toward a student's circumstances. There is a careful balance to being empathetic while holding students accountable.

In order to cultivate a calmer classroom, it is important to embody both empathy and accountability. Throughout this chapter, we will examine how to establish an empathetic culture in your classroom by challenging adultism and teaching empathy. Next, we will explore stages of behavior and practical tips to maintain calm. We will examine why some students reach crisis mode and how to restore calm after a crisis. Finally, we will explore consequences for various levels of behavior and learn strategies to turn consequences into teachable moments. This chapter is built on the premise that an empathetic teacher who holds students accountable ultimately shapes moral behavior, which leads to greater academic outcomes.

The Role of Empathy in Our Classrooms

This work is emotional and requires practice. Think about a student with whom you would like a better relationship. Consider dedicating your reading and research to this student before we begin.

Psychologist Carl Rogers in *Freedom to Learn* (1969) first highlighted the correlation between empathy and learning when he stated that a "high degree of empathy in a relationship is possibly the most potent factor in bringing about change and learning." Furthermore, "When the teacher has the ability to understand the student's reaction from the inside, has the sensitive awareness of the process of how education and learning seems to the student... the likelihood of learning is significantly increased."

Empathy is about understanding someone else's needs and responding with sensitive care. Understanding students' personal and social situations is one aspect of empathy. Having genuine care or concern in response to how students' background, experiences, and emotions have shaped them is being an empathetic teacher.

An empathetic teacher is able to read students' emotional signals because of an already established positive teacher–student relationship (Meyers et al., 2019). Empathy leads to calm. If you are interested in cultivating a calmer classroom, it is important to understand the role of empathy in your interactions with students.

However, empathy is not about removing all boundaries or letting students "get away with" every unfavorable behavior. Every teacher–student relationship needs boundaries. Without boundaries, educators are at risk for compassion fatigue and could eventually become detached from some students altogether (Kasalak & Dagyar, 2022). Educators cannot carry the personal burdens of their students. Boundaries ensure an empathetic teacher does not make themselves accessible to students at all times. For example, every teacher deserves a daily lunch break. There will always be competing interests and opportunities to be pulled in many directions, but it is imperative you eat lunch in a space that is conducive to an actual break. Another example is to consider how you can detach at the end of the day. If you use an app to communicate with parents, check to see if there is a way to turn off notifications during the evening hours. Boundaries are essential in order to avoid burnout. In fact, Chapter 5 is devoted to teacher wellness in order to avoid burnout. In this chapter, we will further discuss ways to set boundaries to ensure you are able to preserve your energy. Empathy is based on genuine care for promoting academic and behavioral growth for students.

The Role of Accountability in Our Classrooms

Students must also be held to high standards of academic, behavioral, and social performance, making accountability necessary for their success. "Instructors high in teacher empathy do not lower standards; they identify and remove obstacles to learning" (Meyers et al., 2019, p. 162). For example, when students do not meet expectations for behavior, an empathetic teacher traces the root of that behavior to understand where it may be coming from. That same teacher also holds the student accountable to their behavior to ensure the student learns the skills needed to repair the harm they have caused and reduce the frequency of that behavior. Restorative circles are a great way to engage stakeholders in authentic conversations to repair harm without shaming the offender. Restorative circles have the potential to be healing for those who were harmed. It takes a skilled leader to conduct a restorative circle, but many schools are moving in this direction, and there are ample resources available to support schools in this process.

Taking personal responsibility is the process of understanding how your own behavior and actions impact someone else. Schools and families should work in tandem to help students develop responsible decision-making skills (Colby & Kohlberg, 1987). Being responsible for your own actions is an acquired skill that requires cognitive development and maturity (Carbonero et al., 2017). This requires a continuous construction of morals and values (Colby & Kohlberg, 1987). Children are still developing moral judgment and the understanding of social norms. A child's development of moral behavior—that is, how they act based on a set of values and standards—is developed by their family background,

home environment, cultural expectations, and how caregivers have modeled behavior (Carbonero et al., 2017) along with expectations set in the
classroom.

That is why accountability is not about slapping down consequences
or removing a student from the classroom when they display unwanted
behavior. Repeated removal damages a student's cognitive ability to construct what responsible decision making looks like. Thus, some students
still need to be taught how to be responsible for their actions and develop
the skills to feel empathy toward their teachers and peers. This is not to
say that we should remove all consequences in schools. That is a misguided
approach. To begin with, ignoring unfavorable behavior contributes to
poor individual, school, and community outcomes (Keels, 2021). However,
accountability is not about punishment. Rather, it is about shaping behavior through teaching emotional regulation skills, which include helping
students own their actions. We will explore practical tools and examples
throughout the chapter.

What Is Adultism?

We sometimes forget that students are often just like us. If they perceive a
threat inside the classroom, they will respond with a fight, flight, or freeze
response. If students feel threatened by an adult, they are likely to escalate. Some students will silently escalate, others may outwardly express
negative or aggressive behavior, and others may struggle to show up every
day.

Adults who desire control of and domination over children may have
adopted the mindset that children should listen to adults because adults
automatically have authority over children due to their age and life experience. "Because I said so" is a common response or mindset of adults who
demonstrate adultism. *Adultism* is the idea that adults place their own
opinions and beliefs over children because they are naturally above them
(Bettencourt, 2018). Adultism shows up in youth–adult interactions (Conner et al., 2016)—more often in urban schools (Bertrand et al., 2017)—and
"can cause young people to feel powerless, disrespected, and dismissed"

(Bettencourt, 2018). These interactions are eminently apparent in schools, where teachers and adults construct students to be dependent upon and subservient to them. Think of a time when a student pushed back on one adult but complied, smiled, and engaged with another. What was different about those interactions and why?

One way to deepen connections with youth is to offer opportunities for students to be a part of school and district-level decision making at various times throughout the year. It is also important to examine our own attitudes using reflective questions such as the following:

- How could students be included in educational decision making?
- What are the opportunities to elevate their voices?
- Why does this matter?
- What do I not understand about my students' experiences at school?
- How could I begin to make deeper connections with my students by engaging in open conversations?

Engaging in reflection about power dynamics, especially from an adultism standpoint, can lead to a reduction in unwanted power struggles too.

What Are Power Struggles, and How Do You Avoid Them?

Fortunately, many educators have developed strategies for dealing with confrontational students. At the top of the list: Never get into a power struggle (McNeely, 2020). If a conversation is starting to move toward a power struggle, find a way to change the channel. You may feel like it is easier said than done. Here are some intentional strategies to cultivate a calmer classroom by avoiding power struggles:

1. Understand a Student's Perspective and How They Experience Life

Empathy grows inside us if we understand where our students are coming from and what they are experiencing. While we were once adolescents ourselves, we have not experienced what it is like to be an adolescent today.

2. Keep Integrity Intact

Confrontation will occur. When it does, handle it privately with the student. While you may be tempted to put your power on display by correcting a student in front of everyone, that only leads to further conflict. Instead, maintain a sense of dignity for both you and the student by engaging in a respectful conversation without an audience. Public embarrassment is sure to lead to a power struggle.

3. Let Some Behaviors Go

It is impossible to address every behavior. Linda Marino, a special education teacher in Mexico, New York, has one method to avoid power struggles. "I have certain students who love to instigate and distract each other, so I made distraction tickets. I give students a ticket when they ignore the negative behavior of another and do not let that student distract them. At the end of the day, we have a lottery drawing with the daily distraction tickets and the winner gets a special prize from me" (McNeely, 2020).

4. Offer Choices as Much as Possible

Choices are a great way to shift the balance of power by creating an opportunity for students to feel like they have control. Choices can shift the balance of power. However, it is still possible to set boundaries by offering appropriate choices. Any time there is an opportunity for students to make a choice, offer them. As students begin to make more choices, they are less likely to feel the need to seek power.

Overall, power struggles lead to more resentment between educators and students. If we want to experience a calmer classroom, we must examine how often we feel the need to be right. Instead, work with students to construct a narrative of school that is centered on valuing students' voices while also making sure the boundaries in your classroom are clear.

Reducing adultism and avoiding power struggles does not mean you are adopting an "anything goes" approach with students. Boundaries are important in every classroom, particularly emotional boundaries. However, applying a "because I said so" mentality is simply outdated and ineffective. Instead, we will examine an approach to managing student behavior built on both empathy and accountability to foster a calmer classroom.

Model and Practice Empathy

There is a strong correlation between the positive mood of a teacher and an increase in a child's well-being. Teacher affective balance leads to fewer emotional and behavioral problems in children (Marigen et al., 2022). Teachers leading calm classrooms understand that the behaviors and attitudes of the teacher profoundly influence the emotions, motivation, attitudes, and behaviors of students (Mendoza & King, 2022). Children, like all humans, are affected by mirror neurons and social contagion. This means that being around a teacher who displays an empathetic attitude will help other students adopt empathy as a part of the class culture.

Empathy is not about letting students off the hook or allowing them to do less because we feel sorry for them. In fact, the opposite is true. When we empathize with students, we want the best for them, and we expect them to give us their best. When we empathize, we meet students where they are, and we understand what they need to grow over time.

Well-being is improved for students and teachers the moment we become comfortable talking about emotions and normalizing them (Ruttledge, 2022). If teachers understand student behavior, they tend to take it less personally, which decreases stress and burnout. Gaining psychological perspective leads to a greater understanding of how to support students, and this empowers teachers to change their perspective of a student for the better. A teacher's willingness to adopt proactive approaches to support student wellness leads to greater teacher wellness too (Ruttledge, 2022). In this way, empathy is good for everyone. This is a good time to recall the student you thought about at the beginning of the chapter. Take a moment now to recommit to an empathetic approach with this student as we explore strategies to increase empathy.

We can use intentional strategies to build an empathetic culture leading to a calmer classroom. Here are some ways to encourage empathy within the classroom (Shim, 2022):

1. Mindful Mondays

To create calm and focus in the classroom, start each week with a Mindful Monday. This includes practicing breathing exercises, meditation, and self-affirmation with students. Students can better calm themselves through breathing and meditation because they have developed these skills with practice (Shim, 2022), which is helpful to draw on mindfulness and self-regulate when triggers occur.

2. Thoughtful Tuesdays

Students focus on kindness and thoughtfulness. They practice gratitude and kindness by sharing messages with other students, staff, and teachers who have helped or done something for them. They can also write notes of appreciation and kindness to themselves. The result is that the recipients of the notes feel validated and that what they do makes a difference.

3. Feeling Safe Friday

Intentionally use this time to engage in restorative circles. This is a time for the class to share feelings in a nonjudgmental, safe, and supportive environment. Restorative circles help students share appreciation, air grievances, or have a directed conversation about a particular subject. This promotes collaboration and understanding between students, reduces stress and anxiety, and promotes well-being.

Of course, even the most empathetic teachers who build safe and supportive environments will work with students who display unfavorable behavior. An educator's goal is to manage the behavior—not fix it. It is ineffective to think your job is to "fix" a student. Rather, understanding the various stages of behavior, from a trigger to a crisis, and being empowered with strategies to manage each phase will help you maintain a calm classroom.

Stages of Behavior Escalation

Prevention

Much of this book is about prevention by intentionally applying strategies to cultivate a calmer classroom. Thus, we will spend time specifically focusing on interventions that can be applied once a trigger occurs. The goal is to avoid escalation (see Figure 4.1) by intervening at the first sign of a trigger.

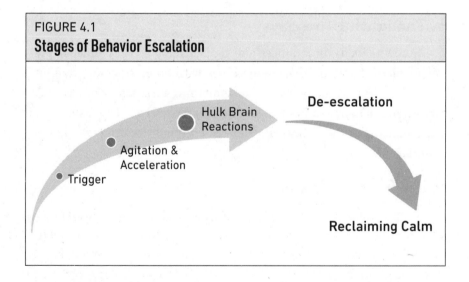

FIGURE 4.1
Stages of Behavior Escalation

Trigger

Many students struggle to cope with mental health distress, often rooted in traumatic experiences, which can cause them to act out. At the same time, other students are silently suffering, and their needs may be unmet because we are unaware that they are experiencing the symptoms of anxiety or depression. Other students are used to "getting their way" at home and have a hard time following expectations at home, often becoming upset when they do not get their way. Additionally, some children are emotionally neglected, often overstimulated by technology and unable to concentrate, which creates tension when they are expected to complete work. There are a variety of reasons why some students are triggered more easily than others.

A trigger occurs when a student experiences unresolved conflicts that trigger behavior to escalate. Sometimes students look for a "safe target" to displace their anger and will act out around their favorite teacher. Focus on prevention or redirection and remove or adjust the trigger if at all possible. Using rewards to affirm safe behavior can help, but remember to make sure the rewards are achievable and the student knows and believes they are as well. If the student does not buy in, the behavior will not change. The little wins will eventually lead to great gains.

Agitation and Acceleration

When a student becomes increasingly unfocused or upset, they may begin to challenge authority and become more aggressive in their body language and tone. However, in this stage, some students may exhibit avoidance or begin to shut down. Students in this stage are often feeling anxiety and need predictability to avoid full escalation (Colvin & Scott, 2014). Consider some predictable routines and procedures that you can put in place to help students feel safe. Think about routines that could be clarified.

It is critical during this stage to use a nonconfrontational approach to help the student return to calm. Here are some intentional strategies to manage the agitation/acceleration stage of behavior:

1. Be aware of body language, tone, and cadence.

Begin by noticing your body language, including how you hold your hands and relax your face. Take note of your height in relation to the students. It may be necessary to kneel or sit to avoid towering over a student.

It is essential to correct behavior subtly and privately as much as possible. Take a deep breath and slow down your speech to give directives that "reduce a student's anxiety and perception of threat" (Keels, 2021).

It is crucial that the student feels heard. You might try different variations of "I care about how you feel. My goal is to help you resolve the problem." While the student needs to admit wrongdoing and accept responsibility for their actions, we have to begin with establishing a safe environment in order to cultivate calm during situations when emotions spike. A student's voice needs strengthening to calm a situation, even if the student has broken a rule or done something disruptive. Doing so will reduce shame and develop social and emotional competencies. It is essential to preserve dignity to ensure students feel safe. Monitoring body language, tone, and cadence will ultimately invite calm into what could be a crisis. Remember, the ultimate goal is social competence for the student. We want students to feel safe so the frequency of crisis behavior is diminished.

2. Correct behavior with affective statements.

The language we use matters. Think about a time when you disagreed with someone and said something a certain way, and it rubbed the other person the wrong way, worsening the situation. Conversely, we have had experiences where we engaged in healthy conversation, had accountability in the conversation, and the situation did not get explosive. Most likely, you used language tools to avoid escalation.

In the first scenario, you most likely used affective language. Affective statements differ from traditional language because they invite empathy with accountability into our classrooms when students need to be corrected. When we use a traditional response like "Sit down and be quiet" or "I am not going to ask you again" or "Stop kicking her chair," there is a potential to activate a threat response. However, affective language holds students accountable while removing the negative emotion associated with the unfavorable behavior. For example, you might say, "When you talk over your classmates, I feel frustrated because they are unable to share their ideas," or "I love your enthusiasm, but please raise your hand the next time you have something to contribute." Additionally, "When you kicked Susan's chair, I felt frustrated because our classroom must be a safe place for everyone to learn. Please stop." These responses are intentional because they invite both empathy and accountability at that moment. You are not letting the student get away with it, but you are not making it worse by using language attached to a negative emotional response. The key to effective communication is to elicit an *affective* response, which helps students understand the impact of their actions. This helps students understand the reason for your request rather than just hearing a command. This is one way we build empathy in students.

Affective statements create a human connection rather than demoralizing students when they have done something wrong. Instead of correcting students in traditional ways, this intentional use of language explains feelings without assigning blame or shame.

Affective statements are built with the following language frame: "I feel... when you... because...." Imagine the difference in tone between a traditional statement such as "Stop kicking the chair" versus "When you kick the chair, it makes me upset because your action causes others to become distracted." Think about a frustrating moment in your day. How could you use a frame like this to restate your expectations?

They can also be used to praise students and model using language to build human connection. Instead of saying "Great job," an affective statement would sound like, "I feel inspired by how hard you are working because I know you are giving your best." The idea is to reinforce positive actions with clear language that invites emotion.

Affective statements will help you and your students remain calm by addressing unwanted behaviors in a nonthreatening way (Bernstein-Yamashiro & Noam, 2013). Affective statements change how we communicate and improve social skills. When used regularly, students gain a greater understanding of others' emotions and their feelings. It is important that adults model how to use language as a tool for inviting connection rather than creating a barrier in everyday interactions with students.

Affective language and statements are powerful tools to reduce adultism and power struggles. They also help build children's vocabulary by encouraging them to use words rather than act out emotions, which also helps them understand the impact of their actions. Properly formed affective statements start with observations, feelings, needs, plans, or requests. For example:

- **Observations:** Start with "I see…" or "I hear…"
- **Feelings:** Start with how you feel, like "I feel disappointed…" or "I feel happy…"
- **Needs:** Start with what you need, like "I need cooperation…" or "I need your help…"
- **Plans or requests:** Start with "Would you be willing to…" or "In the future…"

3. Avoid isolating students.

Many years ago, when I was a new administrator, I noticed several teachers use isolation as punishment. I was shocked to see empty student desks in the hallway, as if there was an expectation that a child would act out and they would need to sit away in the hallway. It was even worse when I witnessed this happen and saw exclusion as a means to punish students who did not follow the rules. As humans, we have an innate desire to belong. Isolating students can do more harm than good.

4. Break down directions into smaller steps.

It is important to scale back expectations for the moment and provide reasonable options/choices to restore calm. Use short phrases and allow processing time before giving another direction. For example, "When you are ready, I would like you to join us" or "You may stay here, take a bathroom and water break, or relax in the calming corner."

5. Use active listening to ensure the student feels heard.

Restate what the student is expressing to show you understand their feelings. For example, the echo effect works well. Simply repeating what a student says can validate that you hear them. If the student says, "I am so angry," you might echo that with "You are so angry." You can also try paraphrasing by using a language frame such as "I heard you say...." These affirm students and demonstrate active listening.

It is important for you to maintain calm and remain detached from the behavior. Remember, this is not a teachable moment. It is also not a time for consequences. This is a time to work on restoring calm to avoid further escalation and crisis.

Hulk Brain Reactions

Hulk brain reactions are the peak of crisis behavior. The goal is to avoid crisis behavior, but at times it is unavoidable. For some students, there are several opportunities to intervene when a trigger occurs to avoid complete escalation. The goal is for interventions to be applied and for calm to be restored. When interventions are ineffective, some students will escalate to a Hulk brain reaction. In rarer cases, a student will go immediately from being triggered to an immediate Hulk brain reaction.

Why are some students more prone to Hulk brain reactions?

Our emotion regulation skills help us restore calm. Emotion regulation skills begin developing at birth. Babies need emotional communication with a caregiver in order to develop healthy attachments (Haft & Slade, 1989). Our brains are hardwired to evaluate tone of voice, facial expressions, gaze, and body posture. All of this leads to our ability to connect to our caregiver. When early interactions with a caregiver are harsh, hurtful, dismissive, or humiliating, the child's nervous system senses harm. If an 18-month-old toddler falls and stubs their toe, they need their caregiver to pick them up, soothe them, and let them know they are OK. This bonding or attachment experience is needed to help the toddler develop regulation skills. Not every caregiver is equipped with the skills to form healthy attachments. Caregivers who experienced healthy attachments in their own childhood are more likely to attune to the needs of a child (Haft & Slade, 1989). *Affect* embodies emotions and moods. Thus, caregivers' affect can greatly influence the child's affect.

When a child lacks healthy attachment experiences, they also lack the development of emotion regulation from an early age. By the time these children enter school age, they may struggle with managing their emotions and become dysregulated very quickly.

Children who exhibit Hulk brain reactions have difficulty with emotion regulation. Think of a Hulk brain reaction as an overblown reaction to seemingly ordinary and even mild conflict (Sayers, 2007). When this happens, we have to remember to stop taking it personally. Rather, to cultivate a calmer classroom, it is important to skillfully respond to Hulk brain reactions.

What does a Hulk brain reaction look like?

If someone accidentally bumps into your cart at the grocery store, how do you react? How does the other person react? Does the situation escalate or a confrontation ensue? Emotional regulation becomes essential in this situation. If someone bumps into me at the grocery store, I do not start screaming at them. However, we have all witnessed overreactions and may have even overreacted at times in our own lives.

Recently, I was traveling to beautiful Puerto Rico. If you have ever traveled on an airline that lines you up based on a letter and number system, you understand that a little communication is necessary. The usual process is people politely going up to each other and asking which number they have in order to line up numerically. It was 4:45 a.m., and we were boarding an early flight, doing our best to line up efficiently, until a guy in front of me yelled at another guy, accusing him of "cutting the line." To my surprise, the two men started going at it over something as simple as lining up to get on an airplane.

This situation is an example of someone becoming easily dysregulated and getting upset quickly over something most people would not normally escalate over. It was easy for me to judge the two men fighting in the line because I thought it was ridiculous. However, when we are empathetic, we take a step back and consider what is happening with the person on the other end. Their reaction could have absolutely nothing to do with lining up for a plane ride but rather a response to something else happening in that person's life on that day.

Our body is hardwired to protect us from stress. Our hypothalamus, the tiny region at the brain's base, sends signals to increase adrenaline and cortisol (Brendtro, 2015) when we feel threatened.

Our heart rate and blood pressure increase due to adrenaline. And our most significant stress hormone, cortisol, communicates with the brain, which begins to affect our mood and feelings of fear. Cortisol also increases sugars (glucose) in the bloodstream (Brendtro, 2015).

Once a perceived threat has passed, hormone levels return to their normal state. However, repeated exposure to stress means children and adults can stay in a state of flight, flight, or freeze because they constantly feel under attack (Brendtro, 2015). That is, the fight-or-flight response remains active.

According to Siegel and Bryson (2011), overexposure to cortisol and other stress hormones increases the risk of many symptoms such as digestive problems, headaches, muscle tension, concentration issues, sleeping problems, and more.

This response is particularly true among adolescents whose emotions are linked to changes in their cortisol levels (Adam, 2006). Adolescents experiencing puberty are more likely to experience more elevated cortisol in response to an unfavorable situation or emotion. Therefore, it is no surprise that changes in hormones play a role in mood states, which also affect cortisol levels. On average there is a 5–8 percent increase in cortisol for every negative emotion, although this varies quite a bit from person to person. Genetic factors can also be responsible for raised cortisol levels in response to negative emotions (Adam, 2006).

An interesting fact is adolescents' cortisol levels are typically higher when they are alone. This research speaks to the importance of adult intervention to help reduce Hulk brain symptoms. As we age, being alone or feeling alone does not spike cortisol levels in the same way levels spike for adolescents (Adam, 2006).

A Hulk brain reaction activates the "downstairs" brain. We can think of the downstairs brain as the place where basic needs like sensory processing, safety, and reactivity occur. It is our "upstairs" brain that helps us to make rational decisions. Upstairs brain thinking happens in the prefrontal cortex, the command and control center for executive functions (Siegel & Bryson, 2011). This part of the brain helps us empathize with others to focus and control our emotions. Our goal now is to help the student access their upstairs brain once again.

How do you de-escalate Hulk brain reactions?

When a student displays a Hulk brain reaction to an unfavorable situation or emotion, the first thing to do is to ensure that the setting is safe and as calm as possible, for both the escalated student and any other students who are present. Find a calm, quiet space to talk to the student when possible. It could be the side of the classroom, a quiet space, or a corner. It is possible you will need another adult to take the rest of your class to a safer location to remove the audience from the escalated student. This may also be necessary in order to keep other students safe, especially if the student in crisis refuses to move to a safe location.

If this occurs, a classroom teacher should not try to de-escalate Hulk brain reactions alone. Safety is the first priority, so be sure to call for help. Remember, generally, you should avoid being alone with an escalated student. However, you also want to prevent introducing too many adults into the situation to avoid overwhelming the student.

Every adult needs to be clear that this is not a time to threaten consequences. The goal now is to de-escalate the Hulk brain reaction and help the student restore inner calm. Having an adult enter the situation and start threatening consequences will only make the situation worse. Anyone working with a child experiencing a Hulk brain reaction should avoid getting in the student's face, using sarcasm, or shouting back.

Instead, use rhythmic responses to reduce anger and frustration, which help adrenaline and cortisol levels return to a regulated state. Try helping the student by stabilizing emotions. We can use intentional strategies to manage Hulk brain reactions and restore calm.

1. Help the child manage emotions by slowing down the reaction.

- Model breathing deeply, and use as few words as possible in the beginning of the interaction.
- Stand slightly angled away from the student (tilt your body to the side so you do not face them directly), and keep your hands by your sides (do not cross your arms or ball your fists).
- Keep your voice calm and your volume low. Use an even tone and keep your face neutral. Speaking quietly conveys patience, authority, and calm, and sends the message to the student that things will be OK. If the student isn't ready to communicate, it's also OK not to say anything and just use your body to be a reassuring presence.

2. Use simple, direct language instead of long lectures. When humans are upset, our brains cannot easily process complex language. Use short sentences, give the student a chance to process and respond, and do not worry if the student does not immediately respond (i.e., don't be offended and think that they are ignoring you).

3. Don't minimize the student's struggle. Avoid phrases that start with "At least..." or "I think maybe what really happened was..." or anything similar. The student very well may be overreacting; for the time being, however, just accept that their perception is their reality.

4. Listen more. Do not immediately try to jump in with solutions, consequences, or advice. Use active listening strategies like asking open-ended questions, repeating back what you hear, and labeling what you're seeing. Try to understand how the student feels and what caused the outburst. Take a moment to remind the student that you care about their feelings. You may use phrases such as the following:

- "Let's see if we can figure out how to take care of this situation."
- "Tell me more so that I can better understand why you're upset."

- "It might help to sit down and take a few breaths. Do you want to try that?"
- "Is there someone else you'd feel comfortable talking to about what's going on?"
- "It's OK if you're not ready to talk. Let's just sit here for a moment."

5. Suggest another activity to do together. For example, playing ball, going for a walk, or another rhythmic activity can help them naturally self-regulate by practicing a rhythmic and repetitive task.

6. Avoid making promises you may not be able to keep, such as "You won't get in trouble for this." You may not know the whole situation, so avoid making any decisive statements. You do not have to agree with everything the student says in order to be supportive. If a student says, for example, "The art teacher was being totally unfair when she told me I couldn't use the clay that everyone else was allowed to use!" you can say something like "It seems like that made you really frustrated."

7. Be patient. Returning to a regularized state may take time.

Reclaiming Calm

In order to reclaim calm, identify the next steps. This may depend on the procedures your school has in place for students who are escalated. The student may need to talk to a counselor or mentor to process the events. Often, a restorative conversation can provide an opportunity for the student to repair harm. Consider when and how parents/caregivers will be notified.

Here are some intentional strategies to reclaim calm after a crisis is over:

1. Reflective Questions to Repair Harm

A copy of reflective questions can be found by visiting the International Institute of Restorative Practices (https://www.iirp.edu/). Restorative questions help students understand their role in harming another person or group of people. After restoring a sense of calm, it is important to help a student understand the consequences of their behavior. These questions also allow time for the student who caused harm to process their feelings and get clear about what they can do to repair the harm they caused.

These questions invite vulnerability into the situation that occurred. They are not only important for shaping and managing behavior; they can also help those who were hurt feel a sense of restoration after being harmed.

These questions are designed to help students articulate what happened from their point of view. They also help students process how their actions affected others and what they need to do next in order to accept responsibility and repair relationships.

2. Huddle and Plan

This is such a simple yet underutilized strategy. Huddle with every stakeholder and create a plan after a crisis or difficult behavior occurs. Huddles are not long, drawn-out meetings; no one has time for that, especially when crisis behaviors occur. When unwanted behaviors occur and the day is done, the adults involved need to lean on each other. A quick standing huddle provides an opportunity to quickly debrief what happened to increase communication among the adults. If this cannot happen immediately after school, ask for a huddle first thing in the morning. A huddle typically lasts 10–15 minutes at most. This is a time to look at the current plan in place for the student and determine if any modifications need to be made. It is also a time for educators to check on each other. When harmful behaviors occur, normalize the fact that it hurts. Allow space to be with colleagues who can provide support and encouragement along with a strategic plan for how to proceed after a tough day.

What About Consequences?

As a young principal, I would frequently hear teachers express frustration that sounded something like the following: "He comes right back to my room without any consequences." "The other students see what she is doing, and they start acting that way too." "My students do not understand why he gets to leave the room to take a break." "Other students see him getting away with it."

Now that I work with schools across the country, I am finding the same sentiment to be felt in schools across America. I surveyed 75 teachers to find out how they really feel about consequences, and the results were quite consistent. Educators are generally not asking for punishment to be placed on students; they are asking for consistency and communication regarding how student behavior is managed. Teachers said things such as the following: "I just want to be included in the conversation. I feel defeated when I am told 'it was handled' but I am never in on what was done." "I feel so frustrated when a student is sent back to my room and I have no idea if anything was done. It seems like they just had fun in the office." "Our school needs to be consistent. Consequences are all over the place and sometimes nonexistent. Most teachers have no idea why a consequence was given—or not given." "I feel alone and almost blamed when a student is sent to the office. I don't send them unless it's absolutely critical, like fighting or another child's safety is violated... so why am I left to feel like I did something wrong?"

As a classroom teacher, some of the practices and policies within your classroom may be out of your locus of control. If your beliefs are so far misaligned with the practices in your school, the school may not be the right fit for you. This will be something you will need to reflect on rather than remaining angry for years because of the factors out of your control. However, most administrators want to collaborate with educators who are able to balance empathy with accountability. When I had a staff member whose go-to strategy was to send a student to the office for every unwanted behavior or if their interactions with students were misaligned to the values of the school, my first concern was to help the teacher understand the balance between empathy and accountability.

However, many staff members were fully committed to building relationships with students, and they were genuinely coming to me to seek support. I loved the opportunity to work collaboratively to examine the complexities of the student's behavior so we could create a custom plan.

Even the best teachers will encounter student behavior of such complexity that it may feel impossible to find an approach that works. Even the best administrators will feel unsure of how to help, even though they genuinely want to provide solutions. In my career, there were times when a student's behavior was so complex that it literally took a team of us huddling daily to coordinate a plan, and we took it one day at a time. But we had to do it together in order to survive and eventually help the student thrive. When educators and administrators work on the same team, rather than blaming each other with statements such as "I wish my admin would…" or "I wish these teachers would…," then even the most frustrating situations can begin to feel lighter.

Best Practices When Issuing Consequences

When issuing the consequence, remove extra language and be mindful of your reactions. Regardless of how upset or dismissive the student seems, it is important to keep your vocabulary simple and your sentences brief. Stick with one sentence. I refer to this as the "broken record" response. At first, the student may ignore you. Avoid letting their lack of response escalate you. If they are beginning to calm down but not yet taking responsibility, use gentle repetition of the command you have given in a soft, regulated voice.

It is important to understand that consequences are meant to become teachable moments, not punishments to get back at a student. It can be ineffective to issue a consequence when a behavior occurs without having planned for the use of appropriate consequences. Often, consequences will be either too harsh or too lenient, because nothing appropriate comes to you in the moment. Instead, examine the trauma-sensitive consequences in this chapter. Be clear on the match between the behavior and appropriate consequences. You can think of this as a menu of choices and use the list flexibly as a guide. It is important to think about the lesson you want the student to learn—and this lesson should be attached to the consequence.

Remember, some consequences are ineffective. Effective consequences should help students make better choices in the future.

Sometimes, it takes a bit of trial and error. And sometimes, behavior problems get worse before they get better.

Utilizing a Salutogenic Approach

A traditional way of thinking about the wellness of ourselves and others is that when something is broken, we fix it. This concept is a very outdated way of understanding people, interacting with students, and cultivating calmness in our classrooms. The idea stems from applying pathogenesis, or the study of disease, to support someone experiencing some type of complex emotion.

Let me give you an example. If a student goes out onto the playground and falls and breaks their arm, they will likely get a cast and, six weeks later, heal. That is pathogenesis, thinking from the perspective of applying intervention to fix or heal someone. Instead, the study of health and wellness is called *salutogenesis*. That is, we cannot fix a situation by applying one intervention. We can start by slowing down.

First, we must recognize that there is no one-size-fits-all strategy. What helped to cultivate calm in your classroom this year may not be the same as next year. *Salutogenesis* is a term that describes multiple factors that support human health and well-being rather than trying to fix behavior using one approach. Applying salutogenesis in your classroom involves understanding that we cannot fix student behavior, but instead we support students in managing behavior using multiple approaches.

You might try a strategy with one student and it worked beautifully, and then you try it with the next student and it did not seem to work the same. We may have to make modifications to the strategies that we try in order to support our students. That is why it is important to work with your team, a coach, your administration, or a mentor to create a strategy and then make modifications along the way.

The next section provides a list of various levels of behavior and suggested consequences. However, a salutogenic mindset is best. Use this resource as a guide. Each student and situation are different. Therefore, this is meant to provide you with options to consider. This is not an authoritative document that is meant to make the process of issuing consequences rigid.

Trauma-Sensitive Consequences

It is important to come to agreement with other school staff on which behaviors fall into Tier 1, Tier 2, or Tier 3. Positive Behavior Interventions and Supports (PBIS) training from the Center on PBIS (https://www.pbis. org/) does an excellent job describing each of the tiers with aligned consequences. Educators from a variety of schools across the country, including my former school, have created similar documents to outline levels of behavior and consequences using the structure provided by the Crisis Prevention Institute under PBIS Resource Guide: An Overview on PBIS Implementation and Resources (2023).

A trauma-sensitive guide to levels of behavior has been added to my website: www.calmerschools/resources.

Proactive Approaches to Frequent Behavior Outbursts

A classroom teacher cannot manage Tier 3 or Tier 4 behavior alone. When these types of behaviors continue, consider advocating for your administrative or counseling team to develop a Behavior Intervention Plan (BIP), which is produced after a Functional Behavioral Assessment (FBA) is conducted. Most school counselors or school psychologists are trained to develop these plans. By working together, school teams can identify the roots of challenging behavior and customize interventions accordingly.

A collection of resources has been gathered to support classroom teachers in understanding how to work with students who display Tier 3 and Tier 4 behaviors. Visit www.calmerschools.com/resources and click on the Padlet entitled "Positive Behavior Support Toolkit."

Consider using contracts to provide clear expectations that are customized to match the individual needs of the student, including rewards and consequences. You may work with a student who does not seem to care about meeting the goals of their contract. Remember, your goal is to ensure the student *learns* from the contract. When a student does not earn the reward on the contract, it is not uncommon for them to respond with an "I don't care" attitude. We have the potential to take it personally when students respond this way. When we take it personally, the student continues to hold the power. Simply put, if you're looking for your student to immediately apologize, it may be time to work on separating your emotions from the situation. The goal of a contract is to shape behavior, but with some students it will take time and consistency.

Here are a few simple steps to consider when setting up a contract:

Customize the Contract

When working on managing student behavior, start small. Some students will only be able to work on one goal at a time. Others will be able to handle two goals, but more than two is overwhelming for most students. The goal of the contract is to shape behavior, and adding too many goals at once will automatically set the student up to fail. As you consider which one or two goals to select for the contract, remember that the more you can use the contract to praise student behavior, the better. So, start with goals that are likely obtainable. Often contracts require students to comply or change behavior quickly. Unreasonable expectations or too many demands have the potential to shame students who are on contracts. If most days the student cannot reach the goal(s) on the contract, then it is time to change it.

Include Student Voice

Students are going to buy into their contract more if they have a voice in creating it. Have students help design the goals and rewards as much as possible. This will vary depending on the student's age, but the point is to invite ownership and build a contract that feels meaningful to the student.

Communicate the Plan

Every stakeholder who works with the student needs to understand the contract, including the child's caregiver. When communicating about the contract, be sure to highlight that its purpose is to help the student improve their ability to regulate and return to learning. It is important that communication is clear and every member of the team feels a part of the student's plan, including their caregiver(s). Clarify what it looks like and sounds like to meet the goals of the contract. This may require modeling the specific behaviors or changes in behavior that are expected as a result of the contract.

You may need to meet with the student for a few minutes each morning to recommunicate the plan. If there is any confusion about what it requires to meet the goal, it is unlikely they will obtain it.

Communicate the Consequences

The tracking method will change depending on the needs of the student. For example, a student who is unable to keep their hands to themselves for longer than 15 minutes should have a contract broken into 10-minute time intervals.

> Describe the rewards and consequences that correlate with behavior choices. Be very specific and clear in this area and use quantitative explanations whenever possible. Involve the parents in designing a system of rewards and consequences. Make sure that the chosen consequences are truly important to this particular child; you can even ask the child for input, which will make him/her buy into the process even further. Have all involved parties sign the agreement and end the meeting on a positive note. (Lewis, 2019)

Follow Up

Regularly meet with stakeholders to assess how the contract is working. This is a time to make adjustments to the contract as needed. Once a goal is mastered, introduce the next one. Eventually, a contract can be removed if all stakeholders, including the student, have evidence that a contract is no longer needed. Regular communication breeds consistency.

Stick with It!

Consistency is key. Over-praise in the beginning. Review the contract and stick to the consequences when the student makes poor choices. Most of all, be patient. It takes time for students to learn how to regulate their behavior. In the meantime, remain consistent and trust the plan.

Examples of various types of contracts can be found by visiting www.calmerschools.com/resources. You may download and edit them to meet the needs of your student(s).

Benefits of a Schoolwide Approach

Implementing a schoolwide approach to positive behavior interventions and consistent consequences may be out of your locus of control. However, it is important to note that a whole-school approach to culture and climate reform can reduce teacher stress and increase student achievement (Ruttledge, 2022). While an individual teacher's self-efficacy has a lot to do with how empowered a teacher feels to manage behavior in their own classroom, the research is clear that positive change is more likely when individual self-efficacy is paired with the collective efficacy of the whole school. It is possible to reduce teacher stress through a whole-school behavior system. You may consider joining your leadership team or working closely with your team to advocate for consistency across your school.

Final Thoughts

Teacher self-efficacy and willingness to adopt proactive teaching approaches are necessary in order to cultivate a calmer classroom. This work is hard. It is even harder when we are defensive and rigid. Instead, use this chapter as a guide to help you customize a plan for specific students who need more support.

Educators cannot be left to manage challenging behavior alone. Draw on the strengths of your administration and your teammates. Be willing to adjust your plan and reset. It is normal to feel discouraged at times. Managing unfavorable behavior can become exhausting. It can be hard to remain empathetic and hopeful when you feel chronic stress as a result of student behavior. That is why it is imperative that you have a recovery plan for yourself.

In the final chapter, we will discuss your wellness. We will examine educator burnout, vicarious trauma, chronic stress, and other factors that can rob you of your sense of calm. In Chapter 5, you will find tools, strategies, and resources for practicing mental fitness. We will have an opportunity to create your own wellness plan based on research and personal preferences. In order to do this work well, you deserve to be well.

5

Regulate with Mindfulness

Imagine you stayed up late to finish a lesson plan and catch up on grading. The next morning you are fully caffeinated and ready to face the day ahead. You open up your email to find that Jullian's mother sent you an email with the subject line "Please Explain." Immediately you feel your body getting warm and muscle tension building in your neck and shoulders. As you read the email you can feel a deeper response in your body. "Jullian said she came to you about Darren bullying her and you did nothing. My daughter should feel safe at school, but you dismissed her. I need you to explain why you are not taking Jullian seriously." You are in shock because the claims are simply not true.

Amygdala Hijack

"Amygdala hijack," a term coined by Daniel Goleman (2011), is based on the powerful influence of a brain region called the amygdala. The amygdala is responsible for primitive reactions to dangerous stimuli causing an emotional response, labeled as fight, flight, or freeze responses. In primitive times, the amygdala's job was to quickly alert humans to react quickly to life-or-death situations in order to survive. Today, the human brain still operates in this way in response to a threat. While we may not be chased by a bear, reading a scathing email can cause the amygdala to take control, and in these moments we begin to lose our sense of logical reasoning (Goleman, 2011).

The 90-Second Pause

Educators face an extraordinary amount of pressure. It is safe to say that we are vulnerable to an amygdala hijack on a daily basis. Most educators desire calm and work hard to establish it in their classrooms. However, it is easy to feel overwhelmed and stressed in our profession because there are constantly competing interests and demands placed on us.

In order to manage the constant stimuli educators are exposed to, self-regulation becomes an essential skill. Overstimulation caused by a constant stream of demands causes an interplay between the prefrontal cortex—the brain's executive center—and amygdala (Goleman, 2011). The prefrontal cortex guides you at your best. The amygdala guides you at your worst. It is important to understand that the amygdala often makes mistakes. While its job is to protect you, the amygdala does a sloppy job determining which threats are real and which are perceived. Thus, emotion regulation is about learning to overcome the amygdala hijack in order to put the cortex back in charge.

When we are triggered, a rush of chemicals puts the body in a state of full alert, causing us to feel a physical reaction in our body. According to Harvard brain scientist Jill Bolte Taylor, it only takes 90 seconds to identify an emotion and allow it to pass (2014). Thus, the moment you notice a physical reaction to a stressor, take 90 seconds to pause and label what you're feeling (e.g., "I'm getting frustrated"). Simply naming emotions helps begin the regulation process (Siegel, 2015). Bolte Taylor (2021) states, "There's a 90-second chemical process that happens in the body; after that, any remaining emotional response is just the person choosing to stay in that emotional loop." It is often our thoughts that are restimulating the physiological reaction for longer periods of time (Bolte Taylor, 2021).

"Name It to Tame It" is a popular strategy introduced by Dan Siegel (2015), who says naming our emotions can help us move from "reactive impulsiveness to receptive awareness," leading us to make better choices when we are upset.

This is not to say that you can dictate what emotions you will feel, when you'll feel them, or even how strongly you'll feel them (Goleman, 2011). The choice comes, rather, in how you will respond. Therefore, the more we can respond to stress, the better able we are to manage these responses.

The Role of Self-Compassion

If it only takes 90 seconds to flush out the body's chemical reaction to stress, then why is it so hard to put this in practice? I will share with you a humbling example. I had a client in California who booked a virtual presentation with me. About a week before the event, the client requested a change to the start time. On the day of the presentation, I was at CVS when I got a phone call asking if I was OK because the session was supposed to have started. Confused at first, I reconfirmed the start time. I was mortified when it finally clicked that the time had changed and I never updated my calendar. One hundred people were waiting for me to start this training, and here I was flippantly looking at makeup in CVS. I cannot recall ever missing an appointment like this before, and I pride myself on being reliable. Immediately, the rush of stress and my thoughts were out of control. I rushed home as fast as possible, flew upstairs to my computer, opened it up, and started the presentation the best that I could. When it was over, I began to spiral.

The event was over, but my body was in full-on meltdown mode. I felt pain in my neck and my shoulders. Actually, I felt muscle tension down to my toes. And then the ruminating began. Every mistake I'd ever made in my life was flashing back in front of me. Self-criticism and self-doubt plagued my mind. I could not seem to recover from the wicked thoughts I was telling myself: "You are not good enough to do this work. You cannot even keep up with basic things like time zones and calendar appointments. You let everyone down. You are unprofessional. You pissed off so many people today and wasted their time."

It took me a very long time to recover—long after the event was over. The embarrassment was too much to work through in 90 seconds. This amygdala hijack was powerful, and it was very hard for me to restore my sense of calm. There will be times when a stressful event requires more than 90 seconds to process. For me, I understood that I was making the choice to remain in the emotional response, in that emotional loop. The thoughts I was thinking were restimulating the physical response (Bolte Taylor, 2021). This happens to the best of us.

I know myself well enough to know I will always feel responsible when I make a mistake. Taking responsibility is a part of being emotionally well. What I have learned, after a lot of practice and research, is that there is still a choice about how we respond when we make mistakes.

What finally helped me heal was self-compassion. Treating ourselves with compassion, kindness, and care when we experience negative events helps us to heal faster (Allen & Leary, 2010). Thus, self-compassion is actually a coping technique built on positive cognitive restructuring. Our ability to shift our mindset regarding how we think about stressful life events determines overall mental health and well-being.

How do we practice self-compassion? We should give ourselves grace and reduce the expectation to be perfect. In the example I shared, I made a critical error. The first step in healing was to engage in self-kindness. Thus, I needed to give myself a break emotionally and shift how I was talking to myself. It is also critical to watch how we are talking to ourselves. Self-talk can either harm or heal us (Allen & Leary, 2010).

The second way to practice self-compassion is to recognize that when we fail, make a mistake, experience humiliation, suffer a loss, or make a judgment, we are actually a part of common humanity and we are not alone (Neff, 2006).

The third way to practice self-compassion is to stop ourselves from getting carried away with negative thoughts. Dwelling on the negative aspects of the situation can force us to stay stuck in a cycle of rumination—continuously repeating self-pitying thoughts and negative thinking (Allen & Leary, 2010). Instead, mindfulness helps us to become aware of our thoughts and consciously put a pause on them (Neff, 2006). When we are mindful, we are able to notice what is happening inside ourselves and take a step back to examine the bigger picture; we can focus on more than the current situation in front of us.

It is also important to note that self-compassionate people are less judgmental of others, which makes it easier to extend that grace to oneself. This is not about denying our failures and shortcomings. In fact, like I shared, I had to take responsibility for my mistake. However, maintaining a loving, caring, and patient view of oneself instills self-preservation and invites a safe space within oneself to admit inadequacies in order to seek ways to improve (Allen & Leary, 2010). For me, I forgave myself and then implemented a checks and balances system to ensure my calendar is set up for multiple clients, in various time zones, with an automated system for scheduling. Thus, my mistake led to growth.

Is All Stress Bad?

Children learn best from a teacher who is happy (Marigen et al., 2022). Happy teachers prioritize their mental health. According to the CDC (2017), "Mental health includes our emotional, psychological, and social well-being. It affects how we think, feel, and act. It also helps determine how we handle stress, relate to others, and make healthy choices. Mental health is important at every stage of life, from childhood and adolescence through adulthood (para. 1)." Not all stress is bad. However, being mentally healthy means we are able to handle stress, relate to others, and make positive choices because we are in tune with ourselves.

Stress is also very personal. What one individual may perceive as a very stressful problem or situation, another may not. While there are many common triggers (e.g., relationship issues, tests/assessments, illness) they also differ from person to person. Let's break down the three types of stress:

- Eustress = good stress
- Distress = bad stress
- Sustress = lacking enough stress

Not all stress is bad for us. In fact, the research says that simply chang-ing your mind about stress leads to a happier and healthier life (McGoni-gal, 2016). A negative view about stress can cause a very negative reaction in our bodies, whereas simply shifting your mindset about stress itself can produce a calmer hormonal experience when managing stress.

Under certain circumstances, stress actually has the potential to enhance our performance and resilience. This is known as *eustress*. Not enough stress in our lives can lead to boredom and depression. This is known as *sustress*.

The concern comes when we experience prolonged or chronic stress, known as *distress*. McEwen (2007) describes the effects of stress over time as an "allostatic load," meaning that stress over time begins to have a long-lasting impact on the brain and body. This occurs when there is fre-quent exposure to stress, an inability to shut off the stress response, and ineffective management of stress (Luke & Schimmel, 2023).

What Happens to Our Body When We Experience Chronic Stress?

Stressors are life events that cause your nervous system to release stress hormones. Cortisol and adrenaline are stress hormones released by the nervous system in response to stressful life events (McEwen, 2004). These hormones constrict your blood vessels, increase your heart rate, and raise your blood sugar, giving you a boost of energy to respond. Cor-tisol is known as the "stress hormone." It is released during periods of stress. When this remains high, due to chronic exposure to stress, it affects everything from performance to ability to enjoy simple pleasures in life. Adrenaline causes an increased heart rate, increased respiratory rate, and changes to the body, which can lead to inflammation, nerve damage, increased adrenaline receptors, and poor metabolism. We call the physi-cal and emotional feelings attached to stressful events our *stress response system*.

Understanding Stress vs. Anxiety

Stress is usually triggered by an event or situation and causes a physiological response (Taylor, 2003). Generally, stress goes away once the event causing the stress (known as the *trigger*) is over. When worries linger for longer periods of time, that could be a sign of anxiety (Fink, 2016). The symptoms of anxiety are similar to stress and may be described as feeling muscle tension or having a hard time concentrating, difficulty sleeping, or increased irritability (Fink, 2016). More often, anxiety is a type of chronic stress response that is elevated, easily making it hard to calm down (Taylor, 2003)—activated but not easily deactivated.

Because stress and anxiety are so similar, the same coping skills and strategies are often helpful in reducing both (Fink, 2016).

It's important to be aware of how long anxious feelings last. A few weeks usually isn't worrying. It's really when these feelings persist for months that it may be cause for concern. When in doubt, talk to your doctor about the best ways to manage stress, as it is important to seek medical help if feelings of stress and anxiety persist.

Stress Management: Prevention

Your wellness matters! Your ability to be well has an impact on both your personal and professional lives. Not only does your ability to manage stress affect your instruction and your students' learning outcomes, but it also can help prevent long-term chronic stress. Studies show that intentional positive interventions can help us manage stress (see Figure 5.1) to prevent memory loss, depression, anxiety, and other negative symptoms associated with stress (Wright & Conrad, 2008). Prevention strategies can help you manage stress, avoid burnout, and remain calm under pressure.

There is strong evidence that stress is best managed by understanding the brain and body connection. First, we will examine the chemical dopamine as a potential prevention strategy to help manage the symptoms of stress. Then we will investigate the connection between our gut health and our mental health.

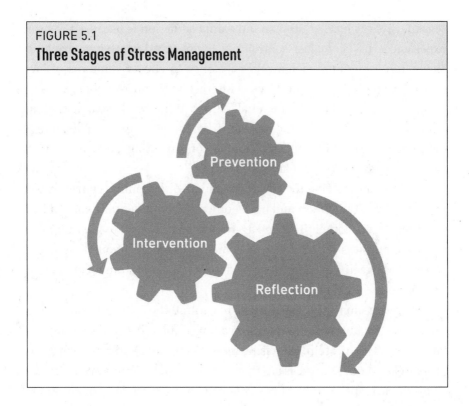

FIGURE 5.1
Three Stages of Stress Management

Boost Your Happy Chemicals

"Dopamine is believed to be the brain chemical that fuels will" (Szalavitz, 2012, para. 2). Dopamine is the feel-good chemical responsible for giving us a healthy boost of energy or motivation. Dopamine is a neurotransmitter that submits signals to the brain that make us feel happy. It is an important chemical attributed to feeling pleasure. When we think about dopamine as it relates to learning, dopamine improves memory and learning. It can also increase our wakefulness and motivate us to complete tasks in front of us.

However, people who suffer from dopamine deficiency may be more susceptible to addiction. Alcohol, drugs, sex, or sugary foods elicit the quick burst of dopamine in order to satisfy a craving (Health, n.d.). One reason why it is hard to stop an unhealthy addiction is because the user experiences psychological soothing, a temporary high, when drinking alcohol or using another harmful substance to cope. Symptoms of low dopamine can cause a general lack of interest in life, apathy, hopelessness, or a lack of motivation (Young et al., 2002). When we have a dopamine deficiency, we can feel fatigue or suffer from forgetfulness, and dopamine deficiencies can lead to obesity, trouble concentrating, and difficulty in completing tasks (Young et al., 2002).

Additionally, having too much dopamine, or dopamine concentrated in some parts of the brain and not in other parts of the brain, can lead us to become more competitive and aggressive and can lead to poor impulse control. Thus, it is important to seek medical support if you or someone you love is engaging in addictive behaviors or if the symptoms of dopamine imbalance are persistent.

There are simple things we can do to naturally boost healthy dopamine in our lives, including decreasing our caffeine intake, eating less saturated fat, eating lots of protein, exercising more often, and getting enough sleep (Young et al., 2002). Music is another way to boost dopamine and cultivate calm. Music helps us connect to our feelings and experience our emotions (American Psychologist, 2022). Even being read to or being told a story is a dopamine booster. That is why many students enjoy when their teacher reads aloud or shares an interesting story to make content come alive. Other simple things like humor, positive interactions with peers, movement, choice, kindness, and gratitude are all dopamine boosters.

Next time you need to boost dopamine and cultivate more inner calm, try writing and rehearsing positive affirmations—positive phrases or statements that we repeat to ourselves. Positive affirmations are a great way to manifest goals, dreams, or experiences we desire.

According to neuroplasticity research, whatever we focus on is strengthened in various regions of the brain (Cozolino, 2006), so we can strengthen our positive neural pathways in the brain by practicing positive affirmations.

My counselor used to start each morning by writing a positive affirmation on a slip of paper and placing it in her pocket. When the day got tough, she would pull it out and revisit her intention for the day. When I started doing this too, I noticed a big shift in my ability to remain calm under pressure.

Positive affirmations might include the following:

- I am getting better and better every day.
- All I need is within me right now.
- I choose to remain calm under pressure.
- I embrace this moment by breathing and noticing my breath.
- I am strong enough to handle what is in front of me.

Additionally, we can manage stress by boosting dopamine using a variety of simple prevention strategies. These are not only good for adults, but they can also be really helpful in cultivating calm in your classrooms.

1. Record Small Accomplishments

Even achieving a minor goal gives us a boost of dopamine, which is why so many of us love to check things off a list! The more that we put our goals on paper and break them down into small, measurable parts, the better we are able to see the progress that we're making. The next step is to celebrate these small accomplishments. Small celebrations boost dopamine. Share your small accomplishments with someone who will provide positive feedback, praise, and recognition, whether it's asking your teammates to start each meeting with accomplishments you are each proud of, simply pausing to look at your listed accomplishments, or engaging in positive self-talk.

2. Stay Focused on One Task at a Time

Many of us love to multitask, but multitasking has the potential to reduce our sense of calm. Listening to a book on tape while doing laundry is not harmful because these two activities do not require concentration. However, when important tasks need to be completed, instead of multitasking, prioritize your activities. Determine the most critical tasks and complete them first. You will be much more successful when you focus on one task at a time, and eventually this level of concentration saves time in the long run. Be cautious when working next to your cell phone. Every time a notification goes off, our brains experience a boost of dopamine. This trap takes us away from concentrating and can lead to frustration over time. Consider turning your phone off or moving it away from your personal space when focusing on an important task.

3. Plan a Task Management Tool

Once you have determined which tasks are most important, put them on your calendar. When you see your task list daily, it can be easier to prioritize your time. You may find that having a visual reminder of each task you need to complete helps you focus better on them. Completing them can also give you a sense of accomplishment.

An Eisenhower matrix is a task management tool that helps us decide what tasks to prioritize, delegate, or eliminate (Bratterud et al., 2020) by charting what is urgent versus important (see Figure 5.2). If we approach everything as urgent, that can cause us to feel anxious and less calm. Instead, a tool like this can help sort to-dos in a manageable way.

FIGURE 5.2
Eisenhower Matrix

	Urgent	Not Urgent
Important	Prioritize	Schedule for Later
Not Important	Delegate	Eliminate

Gut Health as a Prevention Strategy

New research is shedding light on the phrase "gut feelings" by linking our gut health and mental health. Traditionally, the central nervous system has been highlighted as the regulator of our moods and behaviors, but studies are now showing a direct connection between our gut bacteria and elevated stress hormones (Friedrich, 2015). Gut microbiomes, bacteria, can influence the brain and our behavior (Goyal et al., 2015). The human body is host to trillions of bacteria (Wang et al., 2017). Our gut is made up of nearly 50 trillion bacteria known as microbiomes, which are mostly useful but may become harmful when out of balance.

The gut is an essential organ that begins to fully develop within the first three years of life. Our gut's ability to metabolize the various foods we consume can support either cognitive development or cognitive abnormalities (Goyal et al., 2015), and poor nutrition, underrepresented nutrients, or overrepresented nutrients affect children's gut development. Wang et al. (2017) has studied the link between poor gut health and underdeveloped regions of the brain responsible for regulating emotions. Thus, poor nutrition in childhood can impact overall brain health, causing faulty firing in the emotion regulation regions of the brain. Simply put, our gut health affects our mental health from an early age.

This is not just true for children. Adults are affected by gut health too. Diet, exercise, and stress exposure can impact our microbiome health. Thus, the research points to healthy gut bacteria as an important physiological condition that supports overall good health (Friedrich, 2015). In fact, healthy gut bacteria are known to regulate levels of cortisol and adrenaline, which directly impact our ability to regulate emotions (Singh, 2016). Gut health even plays a role in regulating inflammation and our immune system (Goyal et al., 2015). Poor gut health contributes to a slower metabolism and possible weight gain. Furthermore, our gut health is shown to impact the production of serotonin, which plays a role in our overall mood and sleep function. To simplify, think of your gut as your second brain because of the role your gut health plays in mood regulation.

It is important to note that the relationship between gut health and mental health is an evolving area of medicine. However, as research continues to come forward, there are plenty of healthy choices we can make to benefit ourselves.

1. Take in Prebiotics Naturally

Foods or supplements that contain live microorganisms are called *prebiotics* (Satokari, 2020). These are intended to maintain or improve the "good" bacteria in the body (Manning & Gibson, 2004). A diet high in saturated fat and sugars and poor in plant-derived fibers can have detrimental effects on gut microbiota. Fruits and vegetables are some of the best sources of nutrients for a healthy microbiome. Whole grains, fruits, vegetables, beans, and legumes are high in fiber, which stimulates healthy bacteria growth in the gut (Satokari, 2020). Following a diet rich in fruits and vegetables may prevent the growth of some disease-causing bacteria while increasing bifidobacteria, which are beneficial bacteria (Satokari, 2020). Fermented foods such as yogurt, sauerkraut, and kombucha are rich in lactobacilli, a type of bacteria that can benefit your health (Gilliland, 1990).

2. Talk to Your Doctor About Probiotics

Probiotic bacteria lead to improved health (Kechagia et al., 2013). Overall, the term *probiotic* is derived from the Greek language, meaning "for life." They are live microbial supplements designed to improve microbial balance. There is a huge market for probiotics, but it is important to speak with your doctor before selecting a probiotic to determine if it is best for you.

3. Exercise to Improve Your Gut Health

Exercise alters the composition and functional capacity of the gut microbiota. Active women compared with sedentary controls showed that women who performed at least three hours of exercise per week had increased levels of healthy bacteria and improved metabolic health (Mailing et al., 2019). The benefits of exercise on gut health may take time to actualize, but consistency is key in producing changes in bacterial health. Overall, increasing evidence suggests that regular aerobic exercise may benefit gut health (Mailing et al., 2019). It is important to consult your doctor regarding which exercise program might be most effective for you.

Sometimes it is hard to find the motivation to exercise. However, exercise can actually make us happier because of the positive feel-good chemicals that are released as a result of exercise, including endorphins, which give us a natural mood boost; endocannabinoids, which help us sleep better and reduce anxiety; and dopamine, which we need for improved mood and memory (Baloh, 2022). Confidence and self-esteem are also improved with regular exercise.

The brain loves novelty. Therefore, it is important to practice various prevention strategies and change them from time to time. Each new strategy elicits dopamine and will help you restore calm. When the strategy stops working, do not worry. It is normal for the brain to need something new to try. That is why it is important to revisit these strategies and others in order to routinely change how you intentionally prevent stress. Each new strategy provides us with the feeling of hope, and when we have hope, we cultivate inner calm with ease.

When exploring the impact of gut health on mental health, it is important to continue to follow the research, as this is an ever-evolving area of health and wellness management. While prebiotics, probiotics, and exercise are all beneficial to managing stress, particularly when applied under the direction of a doctor, there is new research coming out about the brain–body connection each year. The more we understand this connection, the better able we are to make positive choices for ourselves to manage the symptoms of stress. Prevention takes effort. However, the payoff is the high likelihood that we will feel calmer inside. Ultimately, if we want to feel a greater sense of calm under pressure, then practicing prevention strategies is a way to protect ourselves from the potential harm we might experience otherwise.

Stress Management: Intervention

The nervous system is made up of the *sympathetic* nervous system and the *parasympathetic* nervous system. When we are triggered, we need the parasympathetic nervous system to act as a safeguard reminding us to pause and reset (Dutfield & Lanese, 2019). There are tools you can utilize to stimulate your parasympathetic nervous system in order to restore calm.

The main component of the parasympathetic nervous system is the vagus nerve (Howland, 2014). The vagus nerve can help us relax when we are under stress. We can use simple strategies to help stimulate the vagus nerve to remain calm under pressure.

1. Use Calming Imagery

Guided imagery is a tool used for relaxation. By intentionally focusing on a peaceful scene, we can give our brains a break from the stress we carry (Hart, 2008). Imagine your favorite place. Picture what it looks like down to every detail. Imagine what it smells like and what it feels like when you are there. Allow your mind to escape through guided imagery gives your brain a break rather than focusing on the current stress you're facing (Tindle & Tadi, 2022).

2. Nap

Napping can be a fatigue management strategy. Research shows that a 10-minute nap is the optimal length for when we're feeling a little sluggish and unproductive. A short nap in the afternoon has been shown to improve performance without disturbing nighttime sleep, but be cautious not to nap for too long, as this could result in sleep inertia (Hilditch et al., 2016). Sleep inertia causes grogginess, disorientation, and sleepiness after waking up (Frech et al., 2022).

3. Intentionally Practice Gratitude

Practicing gratitude is strongly correlated with boosting dopamine. The habit of gratitude helps us build self-compassion and self-acceptance, which leads to calm. Gratitude helps us step away from what is causing us stress and shifts our thinking toward others, causing us to get out of our own head at times. You might consider listing all of the people you are grateful for every day for a period of one to two weeks. Or try starting and ending the day by setting a timer for two to five minutes. During the time span, mentally recap the good parts of your day and what you are grateful for. A simple gratitude pause can do wonders for restoring calm.

4. Say No

You do not have to volunteer for every committee or activity. You may choose to use intentional language if saying no is hard for you: "I would like to help, but it is important to me to do a good job. I am just too stretched right now to take on this commitment." It is empowering to say no sometimes. Consider when it is important to say no in order for you to remain balanced.

5. Do Nothing

Without a doubt, today's modern lifestyle can be stressful. Making time for yourself can be hard with work, family, and social obligations. However, it is important to schedule time to do nothing. An overloaded brain is not healthy for you or anyone else you serve. Being still allows your brain to reset. While dopamine can help us accomplish more, we also need to know when it is appropriate for us to do less in order to remain calm.

Stress Management: Reflection

1. Track Behaviors and Possible Triggers

Sometimes it is hard for us to recognize our triggers, but by recording fight, flight, or freeze reactions and the events that preceded the behavior, patterns will emerge over time that will help you identify triggers and avoid them. For the next week, try to record the times of day in which you feel the most stress. When you experience stress, ask yourself

- When did the stress start?
- When did I start to feel dysregulated or uncomfortable?
- What are the thoughts I am experiencing?
- Are these thoughts true or imagined?

Tracing the trigger may surprise you. You may find that you are carrying thoughts from a previous experience with you that make the current situation more stressful. It may be that you need to manage the feelings related to the trigger before you are able to recover from the current stress you are facing.

2. Utilize Music

Music is an incredible way to help us reflect after a stressful situation and even build stamina to remain calm under pressure. Oxytocin, which plays a role in mood and behavior, is released when listening to music. The implications of oxytocin in musical settings continues to evolve, but interesting research is starting to help us understand how music also contributes to a greater social bond and human connection (Chokshi & O'Connor, 2021).

It is also important to pay attention to how you react to different forms of music and select songs that are best in different situations. What helps one person concentrate might be distracting to someone else, and what helps one person unwind might make another person edgy.

3. Cry

Some people are embarrassed if they are "criers." I used to be an embarrassed crier and would apologize for crying. I don't do that anymore, because I realize now that crying is actually really healthy. I have a best friend I grew up with. She had experienced a lot of trauma in childhood, and we were talking a couple years ago when she said, "I can't cry. I don't cry. Because I'm so tightly wound up and the stress is so deeply rooted, I literally cannot cry." And so I said, "How about try screaming?" And she did and we laughed about it, because screaming is one of those things you don't want to do if anybody's looking, and you feel really strange if you do it. But she began to practice screaming, and that was a really great release for her. I've met a few people since then who tell me that they engage in screaming purposefully, rather than crying, because that works best for them.

How Is Burnout Different from Stress?

We can distinguish burnout from stress in several ways. Unlike stress, which tends to be acute and short-lived, burnout is chronic and prolonged. Stress results from an individual attempting to manage overwhelming situational demands or pressures within their environment. Burnout is more likely the result of long-term engagement with a task or situation that has become increasingly difficult. When we experience burnout, it's as if our body has given up trying to cope with the situation; we feel exhausted, apathetic, and unmotivated.

Burnout is characterized by various physical, emotional, and mental symptoms. Signs of burnout may include feelings of hopelessness or helplessness, decreased energy and motivation, insomnia or excessive fatigue, changes in appetite or weight loss, difficulty concentrating, aches and pains, increased irritability or anger, social withdrawal, apathy or indifference toward work-related tasks, and an overall sense of dissatisfaction with one's work (Maslach, 2001). Burnout can also manifest itself through a lack of enthusiasm for activities that used to bring joy and pleasure. As burnout progresses, it can affect your relationships with colleagues and loved ones as well as your performance at work.

Teachers often face extreme levels of stress due to their workloads. Burnout seems to be part of the job. To avoid burnout, teachers must ensure they have enough time for rest and relaxation away from work activities and commitments (Maslach, 2001). It's essential for teachers to manage their energy levels. Engaging in activities such as exercise or mindfulness can help you better control your emotions during stressful times. Additionally, teachers should cultivate supportive relationships with colleagues to provide each other with emotional support during times of difficulty or challenge.

Finally, one of the most important things you can do as a teacher to prevent burnout is remember why you chose teaching as a profession in the first place. You were called to teach for a reason. What was it? What part of the job makes you want to get out of bed in the morning? Is it seeing the faces of your kiddos every morning? Is it the bond you create with them? Is it the impression you leave that will last a lifetime? Focusing on what you enjoy doing most will help you sustain your passion for teaching, even when times are tough.

Of course, prevention is always better than a cure when it comes to teacher burnout. It's essential that educators stay aware of their feelings to recognize signs of impending burnout before it becomes too overwhelming or debilitating. Proactive actions include setting healthy boundaries for yourself at work, engaging in self-care practices, forming meaningful relationships with peers, and maintaining a connection with what motivates you about teaching. By proactively making these changes, you can ensure that you remain passionate about teaching while protecting yourself from experiencing severe exhaustion due to prolonged periods of stress.

With that, you should always be aware of when it is time to get help.

When It's Time to Get Help

It can be hard to ask for help. As teachers, we feel like we are the master problem solvers, the go-getters, and the superheroes. Sometimes we might think that asking for help means failing or questioning our abilities. Nothing could be further from the truth. So, what if you feel burned out and are worried about your ability to reset? It is vital to seek the support of a medical professional to help you adopt strategies for a reset.

While nothing can replace sound medical advice, you might find the following helpful until you can talk to someone:

- Talk with a supervisor about temporary changes to job expectations, possible compromises, or solutions.
- Try writing in a journal. Focus on what you are grateful for and your purpose for teaching.
- Burnout is often due to having a feeling that you lack control. Focus on what you can control.
- Lighten the load. This might mean asking for help at home with chores or at work with general responsibilities.

It is not a sign of weakness to ask for help. Instead, it is a sign of courage. Remember that others most likely feel the same way. When you bring up the subject of burnout and work to find solutions for yourself, you just might inspire others to work with you to find solutions. You never know who you are a role model for.

In Closing

When we become teachers, we are often young and full of hope. We have altruistic dreams of being the teacher who changes lives. I think of my daughter's spirit and hope she will be able to experience joy in the profession. I know, for her, teaching is a calling just as it has been for my husband and me. However, the issues of copy room supplies and school board politics can cause us to become jaded. Just as you would protect a student from being jaded and bullied by the world, you must also protect yourself from the ancillary problems of the job. Yes, it is often easier said than done. However, with intentional interventions and strategies, it is possible.

If you have not been thanked for what you do in a while, please allow me to say, "Thank you for being an educator." I am filled with emotion as I imagine who might be reading this book and what your experience has been. If you have ever felt underappreciated, overworked, or defeated, you are not alone. I have felt that way too. Personally, it takes intentional, daily work for me to stay hopeful. At the same time, I understand that when our work has meaning behind it, there is often a cost. Meaningful work is hard work. What you do every day is more powerful than you realize.

Think about the relationships you have built, the successes you have had, and the connections you have felt along the way. Relish in those moments a little more. Picture them and allow yourself to recognize what you have accomplished. Please know that I am grateful you took the time to engage with me in this way. I hope you are left with a little inspiration and a few new ideas. My heart is with you, and my hope is that you will choose calm every day.

References

115th Congress. (2018). Trauma-informed Schools Act, H.R. 7320. https://www.congress.gov/bill/115th-congress/house-bill/2245

Ada. (2019). *Signs of acute stress disorder.* https://ada.com/conditions/acute-stress-disorderC/

Adam, E. (2006). Transactions among adolescent trait and state emotion and diurnal and momentary cortisol activity in naturalistic settings. *Psychoneuroendocrinology, 31*(5).

Akhtar, N., & Saleem, S. (2020). Happiness and personality traits as predictors of optimism in school and college teachers. *Pakistan Journal of Psychological Research, 34,* 739–751.

Allen, A. B., & Leary, M. R. (2010). Self-compassion, stress, and coping. *Social and Personality Psychology Compass, 4*(2), 107–118. https://doi.org/10.1111/j.1751-9004.2009.00246.x

American Psychological Association. (2021, March 11). *Essential workers more likely to be diagnosed with a mental health disorder during pandemic.* https://www.apa.org/news/press/releases/stress/2021/one-year-pandemic-stress-essential

American Psychologist. (2022). "The social neuroscience of music: Understanding the social brain through human song": Correction to Greenberg et al. (2021). *American Psychologist, 77*(5), 713. https://doi-org.ezproxy.neu.edu/10.1037/amp0001036

Anda, R. F., Felitti, V. J., Bremner, D. J., Walker, J. D., Whitlfield, C., & Perry, B. D. (2006). The enduring effects of abuse and related adverse experiences in childhood. A convergence of evidence from neurobiology and epidemiology. *European Archives of Psychiatry and Clinical Neuroscience, 256*(3), 174–186.

Araminta. (2020a, November 30). *Acute trauma.* Khiron Clinics. https://khironclinics.com/blog/acute-trauma/#_ftnref4

Araminta. (2020b, November 30). *Chronic trauma.* Khiron Clinics. https://khironclinics.com/blog/chronic-trauma/

Arslan, G., & Allen, K.-A. (2021). School victimization, school belongingness, psychological well-being, and emotional problems in adolescents. *Child Indicators Research, 14*(4), 1501-1517. https://doi.org/10.1007/s12187-021-09813-4

ASCA. (2019). *School counselors matter* (research brief). American School Counselor Association (ASCA), Reach Higher and Education Trust. https://www.school-counselor.org/asca/media/asca/Publications/ASCAEdTrustRHFactSheet.pdf

Aupperle, R.L., Melrose, A.J., Stein M.B., Paulus M.P. (2012, February). Executive function and PTSD: Disengaging from trauma. *Neuropharmacology, 62*(2), 686–694.

Baloh, R. W. (2022). Exercise, the elixir for learning. In *Exercise and the brain: Why physical exercise is essential to peak cognitive health* (pp. 89–107). Springer.

Bauer, H., Burno, C., & Millstone, T. (2009). *Increasing constructive behavior of intermediate grade students through the use of the response cost strategy.* https://files.eric.ed.gov/fulltext/ED505022.pdf

Bell, H., Kulkarni, S., & Dalton, L. (2003). Organizational prevention of vicarious trauma. *Families in Society: The Journal of Contemporary Social Services, 84*(4), 463–470. https://doi.org/10.1606/1044-3894.131

Bernstein-Yamashiro, B., & Noam, G. G. (2013). Relationships, learning, and development: A student perspective. *New Directions for Youth Development, 137*, 27–44.

Bertrand M., Durand E. S., & Gonzalez T. (2017). "We're trying to take action": Transformative agency, role re-mediation, and the complexities of youth participatory action research. *Equity & Excellence in Education, 50*(2), 142–154.

Bettencourt G. M. (2018). Embracing problems, processes, and contact zones: Using youth participatory action research to challenge adultism. *Action Research, 18*(2), 153–170. https://doi-org.ezproxy.neu.edu/10.1177/1476750318789475

Bolte Taylor. (2021). *My stroke of insight: A brain scientist's personal journey.* Penguin.

Brackett, M. (2020, May 25). Being our best self during challenging times. https://marcbrackett.com/being-our-best-self-during-challenging-times/

Branson, D. C. (2019). Vicarious trauma, themes in research, and terminology: A review of literature. *Traumatology, 25*(1), 2.

Bratterud, H., Burgess, M., Fasy, B. T., Millman, D. L., Oster, T., & Sung, E. C. (2020, August). The Sung diagram: Revitalizing the Eisenhower matrix. In *International Conference on Theory and Application of Diagrams* (pp. 498–502). Springer, Cham.

Brendtro, L. K. (2015). Our resilient brain: Nature's most complex creation. *Reclaiming Children and Youth, 24*(2), 41.

Bryant, R. (2019). *Acute stress disorder in adults: Epidemiology, pathogenesis, clinical manifestations, course, and diagnosis.* Uptodate. https://www.uptodate.com/contents/acute-stress-disorder-in-adults-epidemiology-pathogenesis-clinical-manifestations-course-and-diagnosis

Burgess, L. G., Riddell, P. M., Fancourt, A., & Murayama, K. (2018). The influence of social contagion within education: A motivational perspective. *Mind, Brain, and Education, 12*(4), 164–174. https://search.ebscohost.com/login.aspx?direct=true&AuthType=ip,shib&db=eric&AN=EJ1204980&site=ehost-live&scope=site&custid=s5071636; http://dx.doi.org/10.1111/mbe.12178

Carbonero, M. A., Martín-Antón, L. J., Otero, L., & Monsalvo, E. (2017). Program to promote personal and social responsibility in the secondary classroom. *Frontiers in Psychology, 8,* 809.

CASEL. (2015). *CASEL guide: Effective social and emotional learning programs: Middle and high school edition.* Author.

CDC. (2017). Mental health. Retrieved October 18, 2023, from https://www.cdc.gov/mentalhealth/index.htm

Center on Positive Behavioral Interventions and Supports. (2023, July). Positive Behavioral Interventions and Supports (PBIS) implementation blueprint (4.0). University of Oregon. https://www.pbis.org/resource/pbis-implementation-blueprint

Cheryan, S., Ziegler, S. A., Plaut, V. C., & Meltzoff, A. N. (2014). Designing classrooms to maximize student achievement. *Policy Insights from the Behavioral and Brain Sciences, 1*(1), 4–12.

Chokshi, V., & O'Connor, D. (2021, August 31). Social touch and our post-pandemic future. Johns Hopkins Medicine. https://www.hopkinsmedicine.org/news/articles/2021/08/social-touch-and-our-post-pandemic-future

Chung, H. Q., Chen, V., & Olson, C. B. (2021). The impact of self-assessment, planning and goal setting, and reflection before and after revision on student self-efficacy and writing performance. *Reading and Writing: An Interdisciplinary Journal, 34*(7), 1885–1913.

Cohn-Vargas, B., Kahn, A. C., Epstein, A., & Gogolewski, K. (2021). Belonging and inclusion in identity safe schools: A guide for educational leaders. Corwin.

Colby, A., & Kohlberg, L. (1987). *The measurement of moral judgment: Theoretical foundations and research validation,* Vol. 1. Cambridge University Press.

Colvin, G., & Scott, T. M. (2014). *Managing the cycle of acting-out behavior in the classroom.* Corwin.

Conner, J., Ober, C. N., & Brown, A. (2016). The politics of paternalism: Adult and youth perspectives on youth voice in public policy. *Teachers College Record, 118*(8), 1–48.

Cook C. R., Fiat A., Larson M., et al. (2018). Positive greetings at the door: Evaluation of a low-cost, high-yield proactive classroom management strategy. *Journal of Positive Behavior Interventions, 20*(3):149–159.

Courtois, C. A. (2004). Complex trauma, complex reactions: Assessment and treatment. *Psychotherapy, 41*(4), 412–425. https://https://doi-org.ezproxy.neu.edu/10.1037/0033-3204.41.4.412

Cozolino, L. (2006). *The neuroscience of human relationships: Attachment and the developing social brain.* Norton.

Derman-Sparks, L., & Edwards, J. O. (2021). Teaching about identity, racism, and fairness: Engaging young children in anti-bias education. *American Educator, 44*(4), 35–40.

DiNapoli, J., & Miller, E. K. (2022). Recognizing, supporting, and improving student perseverance in mathematical problem-solving: The role of conceptual thinking scaffolds. *Journal of Mathematical Behavior, 66,* Article 100965. https://doi: doi.org/10.1016/j.jmathb.2022.100965.

Dorado, J., Martinez, M., McArthur, L., & Leibovitz, T. (2016). Healthy Environments and Response to Trauma in Schools (HEARTS): A whole-school, multi-level, prevention and intervention program for creating trauma-informed, safe and supportive schools. *School Mental Health: A Multidisciplinary Research and Practice Journal, 8*(1), 163–176.

Dutfield, S., & Lanese, N. (2019). Fight or flight: The sympathetic nervous system.

Elhai, J. D., Rozgonjuk, D., Alghraibeh, A. M., & Yang, H. (2021). Disrupted daily activities from interruptive smartphone notifications: Relations with depression and anxiety severity and the mediating role of boredom proneness. *Social Science Computer Review, 39*(1), 20–37. https://doi-org.ezproxy.neu.edu/10.1177/0894439319858008

Erwin, J. (2005). Put back the fun in classrooms. *Education Digest: Essential Readings Condensed for Quick Review, 70*(5), 14–19.

Feldman, M., & Rottman, H. (2018) Transmission: From experience to awareness: Jewish children hidden in France and their children. *Journal of Loss and Trauma, 23*(3), 177–191.

Fink, G. (2016). Stress, definitions, mechanisms, and effects outlined: Lessons from anxiety. In *Stress: Concepts, cognition, emotion, and behavior* (pp. 3–11). Academic Press.

Firth, J., Rivers, I., & Boyle, J. (2021). A systematic review of interleaving as a concept learning strategy. *Review of Education, 9*(2), 642–684.

Fogarty, R. J., Kerns, G. M., & Pete, B. M. (2017). *Unlocking student talent: The new science of developing expertise.* Teachers College Press.

Frech, M.-L., Häusser, J. A., Siems, M.-C., & Loschelder, D. D. (2022). Anchoring and sleep inertia: Sleep inertia during nighttime awakening does not magnify the anchoring bias. *Experimental Psychology, 69*(3), 146–154. https://doi.org/10.1027/1618-3169/a000552 1

Fredricks, J. A., Blumenfeld, P. C., & Paris, A. H. (2004). School engagement: Potential of the concept, state of the evidence. *Review of Educational Research, 74*(1), 59–109. https://doi.org/10.3102/00346543074001059

Friedrich, M. J. (2015). Unraveling the influence of gut microbes on the mind. *JAMA, 313*(17), 1699–1701.

Furrer, C., & Skinner, E. (2003). Sense of relatedness as a factor in children's academic engagement and performance. *Journal of Educational Psychology, 95*, 148–162.

Galbraith, M. W. (2004). Creating motivating learning environments. In *Adult learning methods: A guide for effective instruction* (pp. 141–161). Krieger.

Gillespie, C. (2020, October 27). Generational trauma might explain your anxiety and depression—here's what it means. *Health.* https://www.health.com/condition/ptsd/generational-trauma

Gilliland, S. E. (1990). Health and nutritional benefits from lactic acid bacteria. *FEMS Microbiology Reviews, 7*(1–2), 175–188.

Goleman, D. (2011). Emotional mastery. *Leadership Excellence, 28*(6), 12–13.

Gottman, J. M., Katz, L. F., & Hooven, C. (1996). Parental meta-emotion philosophy and the emotional life of families: Theoretical models and preliminary data. *Journal of Family Psychology, 10*(3), 243–268. DOI:10.1037/0893-3200.10.3.243

Goyal, M. S., Venkatesh, S., Milbrandt, J., Gordon, J. I., & Raichle, M. E. (2015). Feeding the brain and nurturing the mind: Linking nutrition and the gut microbiota to brain development. *Proceedings of the National Academy of Sciences, 112*(46), 14105–14112.

Grote, K. S., Scott, R. M., & Gilger, J. (2021). Bilingual advantages in executive functioning: Evidence from a low-income sample. *First Language, 41*(6), 677–700.

Haft, W. L., & Slade, A. (1989). Affect attunement and maternal attachment: A pilot study. *Infant Mental Health Journal, 10*(3), 157–172.

Harmsen, R., Helms-Lorenz, M., Maulana, R., & Van Veen, K. (2018). The relationship between beginning teachers' stress causes, stress responses, teaching behaviour and attrition. *Teachers and Teaching: Theory and Practice, 24*(6), 626–643. https://doi.org/10.1080/13540602.2018.1465404

Hart, J. (2008). Guided imagery. *Alternative and Complementary Therapies, 14*(6), 295-299.

Hattie, J., & Yates, G. C. P. (2013). *Visible learning and the science of how we learn.* Taylor & Francis.

Health, T. V. (n.d.). *Serotonin vs. dopamine: What are the differences?* Verywell Health. Retrieved April 6, 2023, from https://www.verywellhealth.com/serotonin-vs-dopamine-5194081

Hilditch, C. J., Centofanti, S. A., Dorrian, J., & Banks, S. (2016). A 30-minute, but not a 10-minute nighttime nap is associated with sleep inertia. *Sleep, 39*(3), 675–685.

Howland, R. H. (2014). Vagus nerve stimulation. *Current Behavioral Neuroscience Reports, 1,* 64-73.

Kasalak, G., & Dagyar, M. (2022). Teacher burnout and demographic variables as predictors of teachers' enthusiasm. *Participatory Educational Research, 9*(2), 280–296.

Kechagia, M., Basoulis, D., Konstantopoulou, S., Dimitriadi, D., Gyftopoulou, K., Skarmoutsou, N., & Fakiri, E. M. (2013). Health benefits of probiotics: A review. *International Scholarly Research Notices.* 2013:481651. doi: 10.5402/2013/481651

Keels, M. (2021). What schools need now: Relational discipline. *Educational Leadership, 79*(2), 32–38.

Kim, T. Y., Kim, S. J., Choi, J. R., Lee, S.-T., Kim, J., Hwang, I. S., Chung, H. G., Choi, J. H., Kim, H. W., Kim, S. H., & Kang, J. I. (2017, June 29). The effect of trauma and PTSD on telomere length: An exploratory study in people exposed to combat trauma. *Nature News.* https://www.nature.com/articles/s41598-017-04682-w

King, R. B. (2020). Mindsets are contagious: The social contagion of implicit theories of intelligence among classmates. *British Journal of Educational Psychology, 90*(2), 349–363.

Klein, C. (2022, April 14). *Guiding students to develop a clear understanding of their cell phone use.* Edutopia. https://www.edutopia.org/article/guiding-students-develop-clear-understanding-their-cell-phone-use

Kolb, L. (2017, September 11). *3 tips for managing phone use in class.* Edutopia. https://www.edutopia.org/article/3-tips-managing-phone-use-class

Kopelman-Rubin, D., Siegel, A., Weiss, N., & Kats-Gold, I. (2020). The relationship between emotion regulation, school belonging, and psychosocial difficulties among adolescents with specific learning disorder. *Children & Schools, 42*(4), 216–224.

Korbey, H. (2017, October 27). *The power of being seen.* Edutopia. https://www.edutopia.org/article/power-being-seen

Kryszewska, H. (2021). Glimpses from the classroom: A great way to start a lesson? *Humanising Language Teaching, 23*(2).

Lang, J. M. (2021). *Small teaching: Everyday lessons from the science of learning.* Jossey-Bass.

Lewis, B. (2020, August 27). *How to create behavior contracts.* ThoughtCo. thoughtco.com/how-to-create-behavior-contracts-2080989

Li, Y., & Lerner, R. M. (2013). Interrelations of behavioral, emotional, and cognitive school engagement in high school students. *Journal of Youth and Adolescence, 42,* 20–32.

Liao, M., & Sundar, S. S. (2022). Sound of silence: Does muting notifications reduce phone use? *Computers in Human Behavior, 134.* https://doi-org.ezproxy.neu.edu/10.1016/j.chb.2022.107338

Linsin, M. (2022, April 15). The first step with an out-of-control class smart classroom management. *Smart Classroom Management.* https://smartclassroommanagement.com/2022/04/15/an-out-of-control-class/

Love, J. C., & Langley, N. R. (2020). Exploring educational needs beyond technical competency: Laboratory management, court testimony, and vicarious trauma. *Forensic Anthropology, 3*(2), 82.

Luke, C., & Schimmel, C. J. (2023). Using neuroscience-informed group work with children and adolescents affected by the pandemic. *Journal for Specialists in Group Work,* 1–12.

Lyle, K. B., Bego, C. R., Ralston, P. A. S., & Immekus, J. C. (2022). Spaced retrieval practice imposes desirable difficulty in calculus learning. *Educational Psychology Review, 34*(3), 1799–1812. https://doi-org.ezproxy.neu.edu/10.1007/s10648-022-09677-2

Lynass, L. L., & Walker, B. A. (2021). Building a districtwide safety net. *School Administrator, 78*(10), 7.

Mailing, L. J., Allen, J. M., Buford, T. W., Fields, C. J., & Woods, J. A. (2019). Exercise and the gut microbiome: A review of the evidence, potential mechanisms, and implications for human health. *Exercise and Sport Sciences Reviews, 47*(2), 75-85.

Manning, T. S., & Gibson, G. R. (2004). Prebiotics. *Best Practice & Research Clinical Gastroenterology, 18*(2), 287–298.

Mantooth, R., Usher, E. L., & Love, A. M. A. (2021). Changing classrooms bring new questions: Environmental influences, self-efficacy, and academic achievement. *Learning Environments Research, 24*(3), 519–535.

Marigen, N., Treviño, E., Caqueo-Urízar, A., Miranda, C., & Gutiérrez-Rioseco, J. (2022). Understanding the relationship between preschool teachers' well-being, interaction quality and students' well-being. *Child Indicators Research, 15*(2), 533–551. https://doi.org/10.1007/s12187-021-09876-3

Markowitz, A. J. (2017). Associations between emotional engagement with school and behavioral and psychological outcomes across adolescence. *AERA Open, 3*(3), 1–20. https://doi.org/10.1177/2332858417712717

Maslach, C. (2001). What have we learned about burnout and health? *Psychology & health, 16*(5), 607–611.

McEwen, B. S. (2004). Protection and damage from acute and chronic stress: Allostasis and allostatic overload and relevance to the pathophysiology of psychiatric disorders. *Annals of the New York Academy of Sciences, 1032*(1), 1–7.

McEwen, B. S. (2007). Physiology and neurobiology of stress and adaptation: Central role of the brain. *Physiological Reviews, 87*(3), 873–904.

McGonigal, K. (2016). *The upside of stress: Why stress is good for you, and how to get good at it.* Penguin.

McLaughlin, K. A., Green, J. G., Gruber, M. J., Sampson, N. A., Zaslavsky, A. M., & Kessler, R. C. (2013). Childhood adversities and adult psychiatric disorders in the National Comorbidity Survey Replication I: Associations with first onset of DSM-IV disorders. *Archives of General Psychiatry, 69*(1), 113–123.

McNeely, R. (2020). *Avoiding power struggles with students.* NEA. https://www.nea.org/professional-excellence/student-engagement/tools-tips/avoiding-power-struggles-students

Mendoza, N. B., & King, R. B. (2022). The social contagion of work avoidance goals in school and its influence on student (dis)engagement. *European Journal of Psychology of Education–EJPE (Springer Science & Business Media B.V.), 37*(2), 325–340. https://doi-org.ezproxy.neu.edu/10.1007/s10212-020-00521-1

Metz, S. M., Frank, J. L., Reibel, D., Cantrell, T., Sanders, R., & Broderick, P. C. (2013). The effectiveness of the Learning to BREATHE program on adolescent emotion regulation. *Research in Human Development, 10,* 252–272.

Meyers, S., Rowell, K., Wells, M., & Smith, B. C. (2019). Teacher empathy: A model of empathy for teaching for student success. *College Teaching, 67*(3), 160–168.

Mitchell, C., Hobcraft, J., McLanahan, S., & Notterman, D. (2014, April). *Social disadvantage, genetic sensitivity, and children's telemere length.* PNAS. https://www.pnas.org/doi/10.1073/pnas.1404293111

National Child Traumatic Stress Network. (n.d.). Trauma types. Retrieved October 18, 2023 from www.nctsn.org/what-is-child-trauma/trauma-types.

National Education Association. (2012). Lifting up student voice: *Tips for collecting & reflecting on student feedback.* Transforming Teaching. https://www.nea.org/sites/default/files/2020-09/Transformingteaching2012.pdf

Neff K. D. (2006, August). *The role of self-compassion in healthy relationship interactions.* Paper presented at the annual meeting of the American Psychological Association, New Orleans. [Google Scholar]

Nobel Media. (2019). *The Nobel Prize in physiology or medicine 2009: Summary.*

Offerman, E., Asselman, M., Bolling, F., Helmond, P., Stams, G., & Lindauer L. (2022, March 14). Prevalence of adverse childhood experiences in students with emotional and behavioral disorders in special education schools from a multi-informant perspective. *International Journal of Environmental and Public Health, 14;19*(6), 3411.

Office of Justice Programs. (2020). *Report on indicators of school crime and safety.* https://www.ojp.gov/library/publications/report-indicators-school-crime-and-safety-2020

Patrick, H., Ryan, A. M., & Kaplan, A. (2007). Early adolescents' perceptions of the classroom social environment, motivational beliefs, and engagement. *Journal of Educational Psychology, 99*, 83–98.

Pechtel P., & Pizzagalli D. (2011). Effects of early life stress on cognitive and affective function: An integrated review of human literature. *Psychopharmacology, 214*(1), 55–70.

Perlman, S. B., & Pelphrey, K. A. (2011). Developing connections for affective regulation: Age-related changes in emotional brain connectivity. *Journal of Experimental Child Psychology, 108*(3), 607–620.

Perry, B. D. (2002). Belonging to the group. *Instructor, 111*(5), 36–37.

Rahimi, R., Liston, D., Adkins, A., & Nourzad, J. (2021). Teacher awareness of trauma informed practice: Raising awareness in southeast Georgia. *Georgia Educational Researcher, 18*(2), 72–88.

Rakoff, V. (1966). A long term effect of the concentration camp experience. *Viewpoints, 1*, 17–22.

Rands, M. L., & Gansemer-Topf, A. (2017). "The room itself is active": How classroom design impacts student engagement. *Journal of Learning Spaces, 6*(1).

Rogers, C. (1969). *Freedom to learn.* Merrill.

Rosanbalm, K. (2021, January 31). *Social and emotional learning during COVID-19 and beyond: Why it matters and how to support it.* Hunt Institute. https://eric.ed.gov/?q=covid-19&pg=40&id=ED614459

Rosen, L. (2018). Obsessive/addictive "tiny red dots." *Psychology Today.* https://www.psychologytoday.com/us/blog/rewired-the-psychology-technology/201803/obsessiveaddictive-tiny-red-dots

Rosenthal, R., & Jacobson, L. (1968). Pygmalion in the classroom. *The Urban Review, 3*(1), 16–20.

Ruttledge, R. (2022). A whole school approach to building relationships, promoting positive behavior, and reducing teacher stress in a secondary school. *Educational Psychology in Practice, 38*(3), 237–258. https://10.1080/02667363.2022.2070456

RWJF. (2021, May 11). *Traumatic experiences widespread among U.S. youth, new data show.* https://www.rwjf.org/en/library/articles-and-news/2017/10/traumatic-experiences-widespread-among-u-s—youth—new-data-show.html

SAMHSA. (n.d.). *Substance abuse and mental health services administration.* https://www.samhsa.gov/

Satokari, R. (2020). High intake of sugar and the balance between pro-and anti-inflammatory gut bacteria. *Nutrients, 12*(5), 1348.

Sayers, J. M. (2007). *The Incredible Hulk and emotional literacy: Using superheroes in counseling and play therapy*, 89–101.

Schure, M. B., Christopher, J., & Christopher, S. (2008). Mind-body medicine and the art of self-care: Teaching mindfulness to counseling students through yoga, meditation, and qigong. *Journal of Counseling & Development, 86*(1), 47–56.

Schwartz, K. (2016). *I wish my teacher knew: How one question can change everything for our kids.* Da Capo.

Shim, J. (2022, April 5). 3 ways to boost student well-being and lower stress. *Edutopia.* https://www.edutopia.org/article/3-ways-boost-student-well-being-and-lower-stress/

Shonkoff, J. P., & Garner, A. S. (2012). The lifelong effects of early childhood adversity and toxic stress. *Pediatrics, 129*(1), e232–e2461.

Siegel, D. J. (2015). *Brainstorm: The power and purpose of the teenage brain.* Penguin.

Siegel, D. J., & Bryson, T. P. (2011). *The whole-brain child: 12 revolutionary strategies to nurture your child's developing mind.* Random House Digital.

Silver, R. C., Holman, E. A. & Garfin, D. R. (2020). Coping with cascading collective traumas in the United States. *Nature Human Behaviour, 5,* 4–6. https://doi.org/10.1038/s41562-020-00981-x

Singh, K. (2016). Nutrient and stress management. *Journal of Nutrition & Food Sciences, 6*(4), 528.

Skinner, E. A., & Pitzer, J. R. (2012). Developmental dynamics of student engagement, coping, and everyday resilience. In Christenson, S. L., Reschly, A. L., & Wylie, C. (Eds.), *Handbook of research on student engagement* (pp. 21–44). Springer.

Sriram, R. (2020, April 13). *The neuroscience behind productive struggle.* Edutopia. https://www.edutopia.org/article/neuroscience-behind-productive-struggle

Steinberg, L. (2015). New foundations of adolescent learning: Lessons from behavioral science, social science, and neuroscience. *Independent School, 74*(3).

Szalavitz, M. (2012, May 2). Your drive to compete may come down to dopamine. *Time.* https://healthland.time.com/2012/05/02/your-drive-to-compete-may-be-down-to-dopamine/

Talking HealthTech. (2021, March). *What is cognitive overload?* Talking HealthTech. https://www.talkinghealthtech.com/glossary/cognitive-overload#:~:text=A%20Cognitive%20Overload%20is%2C%20by,the%20amount%20was%20instead%20sustainable.

Taylor, A. H. (2003). Physical activity, anxiety, and stress. *Physical Activity and Psychological Well-being,* 22–52.

Tereshchenko, S. Y., & Smolnikova, M. V. (2019). Oxitocin is a hormone of trust and emotional attachment: The influence on behavior of children and adolescents. *Zhurnal Nevrologii i Psikhiatrii Imeni SS Korsakova, 119*(12), 148–153.

Thomas, M. S., Crosby, S., & Vanderhaar, J. (2019). Trauma-informed practices in schools across two decades: An interdisciplinary review of research. *Review of Research in Education, 43*(1), 422–452. https://doi.org/10.3102%2F0091732X18821123

Time on Task. (2004). *American Teacher, 88*(6), 2.

Tindle, J., & Tadi, P. (2022). Neuroanatomy, parasympathetic nervous system. In *StatPearls [Internet].* StatPearls.

Trauma-Sensitive Schools. (2022, September 20). *Trauma-sensitive schools: A whole-school approach.* https://traumasensitiveschools.org/

University of Colorado–Boulder. (2022, May 10). Rose, bud, thorn. Research & Innovation Office. https://www.colorado.edu/researchinnovation/rose-bud-thorn

Valenzuela, J. (2022, April 1). *A protocol to encourage robust classroom discussions.* Edutopia. https://www.edutopia.org/article/protocol-encourage-robust-classroom-discussions

van der Kolk, B. (2015). *The body keeps the score: Mind, brain and body in the transformation of trauma.* Penguin.

Vasalampi, K., Muotka, J., Malmberg, L., Aunola, K., & Lerkkanen, M. (2021). Intraindividual dynamics of lesson-specific engagement: Lagged and cross-lagged effects from one lesson to the next. *British Journal of Educational Psychology, 91*(3), 997–1014. https://doi-org.ezproxy.neu.edu/10.1111/bjep.12404

Veleminský, M., Sr, Dvořáčková, O., Samková, J., Rost, M., Sethi, D., & Veleminský, M., Jr (2020). Prevalence of adverse childhood experiences (ACE) in the Czech Republic. *Child Abuse & Neglect, 102,* 104249. https://doi-org.ezproxy.neu.edu/10.1016/j.chiabu.2019.104249

Vue, R., Haslerig, S. J., & Allen, W. R. (2017). Affirming race, diversity, and equity through black and Latinx students' lived experiences. *American Educational Research Journal, 54*(5), 868–903.

Wang, B., Yao, M., Lv, L., Ling, Z., Li., L. (2017). The human microbiota in health and disease. *Engineering, 3*(1), 71–82, https://doi.org/10.1016/J.ENG.2017.01.008

Wang, M. T., & Fredricks, J. A. (2014). The reciprocal links between school engagement, youth problem behaviors, and school dropout during adolescence. *Child Development, 85*(2), 722–737. doi:10.1111/cdev.12138

Willingham, D. T. (2021). *Why don't students like school? A cognitive scientist answers questions about how the mind works and what it means for the classroom, (2nd ed.)* Jossey-Bass.

Wlodkowski, R. J. (1983). *Motivational opportunities for successful teaching* (Leader's Guide). Universal Dimensions.

Wojcicki, E. (2021, December 2). *How to engage students in any subject area.* Edutopia.

Wolpow, R., Johnson, M. M., Hertel, R., Kincaid, S. O. (2009). *The heart of learning and teaching: Compassion, resiliency, and academic success.* Washington State Office of Superintendent of Public Instruction Compassionate Schools.

Won, S., Wolters, C. A., & Mueller, S. A. (2018). Sense of belonging and self-regulated learning: Testing achievement goals as mediators. *Journal of Experimental Education, 86*(3), 402–418.

Woolf, N. (n.d.). 2x10 relationship building: How to do it (and why it works!). *Panorama Education.* https://www.panoramaed.com/blog/2x10-relationship-building-strategy

Wright, R. L., & Conrad, C. D. (2008). Enriched environment prevents chronic stress-induced spatial learning and memory deficits. *Behavioural Brain Research, 187*(1), 41–47.

Young, R. M., Lawford, B. R., Noble, E. P., Kann, B., Wilkie, A., Ritchie, T., ... & Shadforth, S. (2002). Harmful drinking in military veterans with post-traumatic stress disorder: Association with the D2 dopamine receptor A1 allele. *Alcohol and Alcoholism, 37*(5), 451–456.

Zeeman, R. D. (2006). Glasser's choice theory and Purkey's invitational education—Allied approaches to counseling and schooling. *Journal of Invitational Theory and Practice, 12*, 46–51.

Zhang, S., Feng, R., Fu, Y.-N., Liu, Q., He, Y., Turel, O., & He, Q. (2022). The bidirectional relationship between basic psychological needs and meaning in life: A longitudinal study. *Personality & Individual Differences, 197*. https://doi-org.ezproxy.neu.edu/10.1016/j.paid.2022.111784

Index

The letter *f* following a page locator denotes a figure.

About the Author

Meredith McNerney is a former principal, speaker, author, and teacher. She formerly served as the principal of a Title I school of nearly 900 students in Montgomery County, Maryland, where 85 percent of students qualified for free meals and 78 percent spoke English as their second language. Before taking over in 2016, her school was among the lowest performing across 134 elementary schools in the district. Under her leadership, her school was ranked as a 4-star school according to the Maryland School Report Card, most notably due to student achievement and growth data.

Meredith and her team utilized an integrated approach to school reform to maximize structures and processes, including accountability frameworks and best practices for promoting social-emotional health while raising student achievement. Reform efforts included teaching students in their first language through a Spanish bilingual/biliteracy program.

As a trained mindfulness coach, Meredith led her school to implement in-person and online mindfulness practices, including mindful spaces and daily schoolwide habits. Today Meredith works with schools and businesses across the country to teach others how to cultivate calmer environments by implementing trauma-informed care. She also teaches courses for educator recertification on mental health literacy, creating a trauma-informed school culture and climate, and welcoming newcomers with a trauma-sensitive mindset.

Meredith earned a bachelor's degree in Elementary Education from East Carolina University and completed her Master of Education as a reading specialist at Towson University. She is currently in a doctoral program at Northeastern University, where she studies the mental health of Black and Brown educators. Meredith lives in Ijamsville, Maryland, with her husband Mark, who is a middle school teacher, and two children, Danielle and Kaitlyn. Visit her website at www.choosecalm.com.

Related ASCD Resources

At the time of publication, the following resources were available (ASCD stock numbers in parentheses).

Amplify Student Voices: Equitable Practices to Build Confidence in the Classroom by AnnMarie Baines, Diana Medina, and Caitlin Healy (#122061)

Better Behavior Practices (Quick Reference Guide) by Dominique Smith, Nancy Frey, Douglas Fisher, and Lee Ann Jung (#QRG120049)

Building a Positive and Supportive Classroom (Quick Reference Guide) by Julie Causton and Kate MacLeod (#QRG120098)

The Classroom Behavior Manual: How to Build Relationships with Students, Share Control, and Teach Positive Behaviors by Scott Ervin (#122033)

From Behaving to Belonging: The Inclusive Art of Supporting Students Who Challenge Us by Julie Causton and Kate MacLeod (#121011)

From Stressed Out to Stress Wise: How You and Your Students Can Navigate Challenges and Nurture Vitality by Abby Wills, Anjali Deva, and Niki Saccareccia (#123004)

Research-Based Strategies to Ignite Student Learning: Insights from Neuroscience and the Classroom, Revised and Expanded Edition by Judy Willis and Malana Willis (#120029)

Teach for Authentic Engagement by Lauren Porosoff (#123045)

We Belong: 50 Strategies to Create Community and Revolutionize Classroom Management by Laurie Barron and Patti Kinney (#122002)

Why Are We Still Doing That? Positive Alternatives to Problematic Teaching Practices by Pérsida Himmele and William Himmele (#122010)

For up-to-date information about ASCD resources, go to www.ascd.org. You can search the complete archives of *Educational Leadership* at www.ascd.org/el. To contact us, send an email to member@ascd.org or call 1-800-933-2723 or 703-578-9600.